COMPLETE ENGLISH

by

E. G. THORPE B.A.

BOOK ONE

Illustrated by

EDWARD OSMOND

D1579266

Heinemann Educational Publishers
Halley Court, Jordan Hill, Oxford OX2 8EJ
a division of Reed Educational & Professional Publishing Ltd

MELBOURNE   AUCKLAND
FLORENCE   PRAGUE   MADRID   ATHENS
SINGAPORE   TOKYO   SAO PAULO
CHICAGO   PORTSMOUTH (NH)   MEXICO
IBADAN   GABORONE   JOHANNESBURG
KAMPALA   NAIROBI

ISBN 0 435 01885 X

First published 1962
96 97 98 23 22 21

By the same author

Complete English
INTRODUCTORY BOOK
BOOKS ONE TO FIVE

Separate Keys are available
for each book

Junior Dictionary
Illustrated Junior Dictionary

Produced by Mandarin Offset
Printed by Scotprint Ltd, Musselburgh, Scotland

Preface

This five-book English Course covers the following Junior School English: Comprehension, Language and Research (Spelling, Vocabulary, Dictionary work and Topics). It is intended for the consideration of teachers who believe that pupils come to school to work to the limit of their ability, that they should enjoy so doing through the provision of interesting work and that they should be encouraged to find out for themselves as far as possible by confident use of dictionary, atlas, reference books, etc.

Book I is for 1st Year Junior quicker pupils and 2nd Year slower pupils. There are thirty exercises, each divided into three parts: Comprehension, Language and Find Out.

Part I, *Comprehension* ("Questions about the Story/Poem"), has two sections: A (fairly easy), and B (more difficult).

The aim has been to present interesting, well-written passages of prose and poetry from a wide variety of authors and to set questions which require thought on the pupil's part.

The number of questions is increased halfway through the book, from A6, B8 to A8, B8.

Part II, *Language* ("Working with Words"), arises as far as possible from the Comprehension passage. The essential points of Grammar at this stage are covered, with constant revision throughout. Particular attention is given to common grammatical and spelling errors, increase of vocabulary and increased facility in the use of Language.

Part III, *Find Out*. Emphasis is laid on common errors, spelling, vocabulary and use of a dictionary, together with simple research. There are four sections: (i) Words which cause confusion (homonyms, similar spelling, etc.). (ii) Dictionary work. The words when found should be used in "own sentences". (iii) Research on a topic connected with the Comprehension passage. (iv) Vocabulary research.

The main topics dealt with in Parts II and III of each exercise are listed in summary form on the contents pages.

"Key to Complete English Book One" is available, giving answers to the Comprehension and Language section, together with some additional notes.

Acknowledgments

Thanks are due to the following authors, or their representatives and publishers, for permission to quote copyright material:

University of London Press for *The First Race* from "Dobbo" by E. G. Thorpe; *Left All Alone* from "The Little Brown Bird" by Elizabeth Clark; *Thomas and Jascha* from "Jascha" by Franz Hutterer.

James Nisbet and Co. Ltd. for *Learning to Swim* from "The Wandering Otter" by Stella Mead.

Hamish Hamilton Ltd. for *A Bedtime Game* from "The Lifeboat Fish" by Dora Broome.

Oxford University Press for *The Red-Cap Gnomes* from "Traditional Tales" by E. Lucia Turnbull; *The Girl and the Skylark* from "The Skylark" by Leila Berg.

The Society of Authors for *Winter Song* by Katherine Mansfield; *The Magic Skipping-Rope* from "Forty Good-night Tales" by Rose Fyleman.

Mrs Amabel Williams-Ellis and Blackie & Son Ltd. for *Fifty Red Caps* from "Fairy Tales from the British Isles."

Macmillan & Co. Ltd. for *Market-Day* from "Story of Holly and Ivy" by Rumer Godden.

Thomas Nelson & Sons Ltd. for *The Old Man and His Wife* from "Old Peter's Russian Tales" by Arthur Ransome.

Blackie & Son Ltd. for *A Young Rabbit's Adventures* from "Our Wondrous World" by P. A. Barons; *Robin Hood* from "Greenwood Tales" by Dorothy King.

Longmans, Green & Co. Ltd. for *Stealing Rice* from "Story Time in the Zoo" by R. K. and M. I. R. Polkinghorne.

Cassell & Co. Ltd. for *Catching Dwarfs* from "Fairy Tales of Germany" by Barbara Ker Wilson.

The Richmond and Twickenham Times for *The Journey* by Aidan Clarke.

Faber & Faber Ltd. for *Tim Rabbit Meets a Stranger* from "Ten Tales of Tim Rabbit" by Alison Uttley.

Hutchinson & Co. Ltd. for *David's Secret* from "Foxy" by John Montgomery.

Contents

5

1

The First Race

It was time for the first race. The race-horses were ready to start.

Whish, whoosh! Away ran Dobbo to join them.

The race-horses were just starting. Farmer Smith shouted. All the people shouted. Some people laughed. Bill the Bull looked over the fence and laughed. Dobbo took no notice. He was a race-horse now.

The race-horses ran like the wind. How fast they ran! Poor Dobbo was left far behind. He could not catch them. He ran as fast as he could, but he could not catch them.

His heart went thump, thump, thump. He was out of breath. His legs ached. Oh, how tired he was!

At last he came to a stop, a long way behind the other horses. He could hear people laughing at him.

"Just look at that cart-horse," they said. "He thinks he is a race-horse. How silly he is!"

Then Dobbo knew he would never be a race-horse. He was too big and heavy. He was only a cart-horse. He would never be really important.

From *Dobbo* by E. G. Thorpe

Questions about the Story

A1. Which race was it:

the first, second, third or last?

2. Dobbo was a (bull, horse, cat, farmer). Which?

3. The farmer's name was Mr. (Jones, Bull, Smith, Bill). Which?

4. What did the people do?

5. What did the bull do?

6. Why did Dobbo run after the race-horses? Choose one of these answers:

He felt frisky. His master told him to run. He wanted to be a race-horse.

B1. Which kind of horse was Dobbo:

a race-horse, a cart-horse, a Shetland pony or a circus horse?

2. (a) Who ran fast?   (b) Who ran slowly?

3. Why could Dobbo not run as fast as the race-horses?

4. Why did everyone laugh at Dobbo?

5. Why do you think it was very unkind of them to laugh at him?

6. Who do you think was Dobbo's owner?

7. Why do you think Dobbo thought the race-horses were very important?

8. What do these words mean:

fence, Dobbo took no notice, ran like the wind, left far behind, ached, heavy, important?

Remember always: If you do not know the meaning of a word, try to find it in your dictionary.

Working with Words

I. SENTENCES

A sentence begins with a CAPITAL LETTER and ends with a FULL STOP. Here are two sentences:

It was time for the first race. The race-horses were ready to start.

Write these sentences, putting in the missing capital letters and full stops:

(i) the race-horses were just starting
(ii) cats chase mice
(iii) foxes are very fierce

2. HERE and HEAR

Here is our new pet.
I can't *hear* what you are saying.
Remember: HERE is a place.   HEAR is what we do with our EARS.
Put *here* or *hear* into these sentences:

(i) Can you —— someone whistling?
(ii) Come —— at once!
(iii) Tell me if you —— a noise.

3. *Spelling*

Spell this day: S . . day   Spell this month: Sep . . . . . .
Write this properly: He s . . d he would tr . harder.

4. What do we call a baby horse and a horse's home?

5. Pick out the right words from the words in the brackets:

(i) Horses, cows and sheep are (birds, animals, trees, people).
(ii) A cart-horse is big and (thin, heavy, fast, fierce).
(iii) We laugh when we are (sad, tired, happy, asleep).
(iv) The wind (runs, walks, blows, climbs) hard.

6. Read these words: begin   finish   stupid   quick

Which word means the same as (i) end   (ii) silly   (iii) fast   (iv) start?

7. *Puzzle:*   Find an animal:

blue   cuckoo   lamb   shop   school

8. Which one is the biggest or strongest in each set:

   (i) the wind, a breeze or a gale?
   (ii) a cart-horse, a pony or a mouse?
   (iii) a calf, a bull or a rabbit?

9. Which is the right word?

   (i) We (was, were) late this morning.
   (ii) I (saw, seen) the accident.
   (iii) John (ran, run) all the way to school.

10. Use these words in a sentence of your own: over the fence

   Here is one: The boy climbed over the fence and ran away.

Find Out

1. Find out what these words mean:

   shout, whisper, chatter
   book, cook, hook, look, rook, took
   The *tired* horse *tried* hard.
   Your *left* hand, He *left* a parcel.
   were, where

   Use one word from each group in sentences of your own, like this:

   ROOK: A big, black rook was sitting on the gate.

2. *Dictionary Work*
   Find these words in your dictionary, then write down the page-number of each one and the meaning given there:

   acorn, address, aeroplane, afraid, angry, apple, arrow, asleep, aunt, awake.

3. ON THE FARM
   Make a list of farm-animals and farm-birds.

4. "Away *ran* Dobbo to join them."
   Make a list of words about MOVING, like *run, hop, jump*.
   Describe each way of moving.

2

Poor Thumbelina

All that summer Thumbelina lived alone in the big wood. She made a bed from blades of grass and hung it up under a big leaf, which kept off the rain. She ate honey from the flowers and drank the dew which she found every morning on their petals.

So summer and autumn passed by and winter came—the long, cold winter. All the birds which had sung so sweetly flew away. The big leaf which she had been living under shrivelled up into a dead yellow stalk.

She felt dreadfully cold. All her clothes were torn. Poor little Thumbelina, she was so tiny and delicate that she was nearly frozen.

Then it began to snow. Every snowflake which fell on her was like a whole shovelful on us, for we are big but she was no bigger than your thumb. She wrapped herself in a dead leaf but it did not warm her. She shivered with cold.

From *Hans Andersen's Fairy Tales*

Questions about the Story

A 1. Thumbelina was (a giant, big, very tiny, a flower). Which?

2. Where did she live?

3. What was her bed made from?

4. Where was her bed?

5. What did she eat and drink?

6. Why was she called Thumbelina?

B 1. Who lived with Thumbelina?

2. (a) What kept her bed dry in rainy weather in the summer?
   (b) Why did it not keep it dry in winter?

3. Why did the birds fly away?

4. Why did the big leaf turn yellow?

5. How tall was Thumbelina?

6. Why did each tiny snowflake nearly bury her?

7. When she wrapped herself in a dead leaf, why did it not warm her?

8. What is the meaning of:

blades of grass, honey, dew, petals, passed by, shrivelled up (wrink . . . or shr . . k), stalk, dreadfully cold, delicate (not str . . . ; w . . k), shovelful, wrapped herself?

Working with Words

1. Write these sentences, putting in capital letters and full stops:

    (i) poor little Thumbelina lived all by herself
    (ii) in autumn the leaves fall off the trees

2. OPPOSITES

    The *big* wood   The *small* wood   big, small: OPPOSITES
    What is the opposite of a *long* walk? Answer: a *short* walk

    Write down the opposite of:

    a *wet* towel, *happy* children, a *rich* man, early.

3. TO, TWO and TOO

    We went *to* the park *to* play football.
    Two boys were fighting.
    It was *too* cold on the hill.

    Remember: TO play, TO the park, go TO school.
    　　　　　　The number 2 is TWO.
    　　　　　　TOO cold, TOO much, TOO hard.

    Put *to, two* or *too* into these sentences:

    (i) Our cat has —— little kittens.
    (ii) Do not drink —— fast.
    (iii) Are you coming out —— play?
    (iv) I am trying —— learn —— swim.

4. *Puzzle:* Find a month:

    summer   February   winter   Wednesday

5. Put *here* or *hear* into these sentences:

    (i) Thumbelina does not live —— now.
    (ii) I can —— the sparrows chattering on the roof.
    (iii) I know you have hidden the book over ——.

6. *Spelling*

    months: Sep . . . . . .   Oct . . . .   days: S . . . . .   M . . day
    My br . . . . . is twelve years old.

7. Which is the smallest:

    (i) a thumb, a leg, an arm or a foot?

    (ii) an elephant, an ant, a rat or a fox?

    (iii) a bluebell, an oak-tree, a bush or a hedge?

8. What is the difference between a wood, a forest and an orchard?

9. ALL ARE WHAT?

Say what they all are on each line, like this:

    owl, robin, crow, wren: BIRDS

    daffodil, crocus, rose, snowdrop

    January, February, March, April

    Monday, Tuesday, Wednesday, Thursday

    yellow, red, blue, green

    apples, oranges, pears, bananas

10. Use these words in a sentence: in a big wood

Find Out

1. Find out what these words mean:

    I *made* a snowman. The lady's *maid*   by, buy

    grass, glass, glasses(2 meanings)   a stalk, a stork

    bold, cold, fold(2), gold, hold(2), sold, told, old

    a *whole* shovelful, down a rabbit-*hole*

Use one word from each group in sentences of your own.

2. *Dictionary Work*

Find these words in your dictionary, then write down the page-number of each one and the meaning given there:

    baby, bacon, bald, balloon, banana, bandage, beach, beech, branch, breakfast.

3. THE WEATHER

Make a list of different kinds of weather, like rain and frost.

4. "All the birds which had *sung* so sweetly flew away."

Make a list of MOUTH-NOISES, like singing. Describe each noise.

Hansel and Gretel

There was once a poor woodcutter who had two children, Hansel and Gretel. They lived in the middle of a big forest. Their father warned them not to go too far away or they would get lost.

Hansel was very clever. He used to drop pebbles as they walked, so that they could find their way home again. But one day, instead of dropping pebbles, he dropped bread-crumbs and the hungry birds flew down and ate them all.

The children could not find their way home. They were lost. They wandered on and on, further into the wood.

Suddenly they saw a red and blue bird which seemed to be waiting for them. They ran towards it, but each time that they thought they could catch it, it fluttered on a little further.

"Do not follow it any more!" cried Gretel at last, but Hansel would not listen. He ran on, and so Gretel ran after him, deeper and deeper into the wood.

From *Grimm's Fairy Tales*

Questions about the Story

A 1. What work did the children's father do?
2. Where did this family live?
3. Who was clever: the boy or the girl?
4. Why did Hansel drop pebbles?
5. What happened to the bread-crumbs?
6. What did the gaily-coloured bird do?

B 1. Why did the children's father tell them to stay near the cottage?
2. How many brothers and sisters did Hansel and Gretel have?
3. What did Hansel do which was NOT clever? Why was it silly?
4. Why did the two children lose their way?
5. Why do you think the pretty bird was waiting?
6. Why do you think Gretel wanted to stop following the bird?
7. Why do you think Hansel would not listen?
8. What is the meaning of: warned them, very clever, pebbles, wandered on and on, it fluttered, deeper and deeper?

Working with Words

1. What is the opposite of:

   a *poor* lady, I have *lost* a penny, flew *down*, a *loud* noise, the *right* way, Please *come*?

2. A or AN

   a poor woodcutter   an apple   a piece of pie   an old man

   We should find it hard to say *a apple* or *a old man*, so we say AN.

   Remember: We put AN in front of words starting with these letters:

        a   e   i   o   u

   (except some special words which you will learn later).

      an animal, an elephant, an inkwell, an orange, an umbrella

   The letters a, e, i, o, u are called VOWELS.

   Put *a* or *an* in front of these words:

      rabbit, ant, bee, fox, rainy day, island

3. Put *to*, *two*, or *too* into these sentences:

   (i) My aunt and uncle have —— children.

   (ii) My father is taking me —— a football match.

   (iii) It is —— wet —— play in the garden.

4. *Puzzle:* Find a boy's name: Margaret   Susan   Peter   Sally   Jean

5. AS and HAS

   Come *as* soon *as* you can.   Sally *has* a new pen.

   Remember: HAS means to HAVE something.

   Put *as* or *has* into these sentences:

   (i) Your dog —— broken down our flowers.

   (ii) —— Peter gone home?

   (iii) Racing pigeons can fly —— fast —— the wind.

6. A woodcutter chops down trees and cuts up wood.
   What do we call the men who do these jobs:

   bring our letters; direct traffic; sell meat; put out fires; sell cabbages, potatoes and carrots; sell tea, sugar and bacon?

7. *Spelling*

    months: Oc . . . . . Nov . . . . . days: M . . . . . Tu . . day

    I   e . . my dinner slowly   ev . . . day.

8. groan   large   snatch   halt   bright

    Which word means (1) grab   (2) shining   (3) big   (4) moan   (5) stop?

9. What are the missing words?

            Alan is a boy: Christine is a ——
     Mr. Smith is a man: Mrs. Smith is a ——
          feet in shoes: hands in ——
       giraffes are tall: dwarfs are ——
         ice is cold: fire is ——

10. Use these words in a sentence of your own: hungry birds

Find Out

1. Find out what these words mean:

    not, knot   where, were   warn, warm   walk, talk
    One day, We *won* the game.   blue, blew
    We *saw* a bird.   Use a sharp *saw*.   A *sore* finger

    Use six of these words in sentences of your own.

2. *Dictionary Work*

    Find these words in your dictionary, then write down the page-number of each one and the meaning given there:

    cabbage, calf, camp, cap, chair, chalk, cheap, chimney, cot, cuckoo.

3. RELATIONS

    Make a list of relations, like father and uncle.

4. "Suddenly they *saw* a red and blue bird . . . "

    Think of other words about SEEING, like peeping and staring.
    Describe each way of seeing.

Learning to Swim

Tibby Otter and his three brothers were born on a windy March day.

Their home in a hole by the river bank was very dark. But Tibby and his brothers did not mind, because otters are blind till they are about ten days old.

When at last the little otters opened their eyes, their mother made a path up the river bank and took them out for an airing.

"My dears," she said, "it is time you learned to swim. Today your father and I will give you your first swimming lesson."

Tibby learned to swim very quickly. His mother swam with him on her back far out into the river. Then all at once she dived under the water.

Poor Tibby splashed and struggled, and seemed afraid of the water. But his father and mother were both there to help him, and soon he was able to swim and dive without fear.

From *The Wandering Otter* by Stella Mead

Questions about the Story

A 1. When were the baby otters born?

   2. Where did they live?

   3. How long are baby otters blind?

   4. What did their mother tell them one day?

   5. How long do you think Tibby Otter took to learn to swim?

   6. Where did his mother take him on her back?

B 1. How many baby otters were there?

   2. Why was their home very dark?

   3. Why did the baby otters not worry about the darkness?

   4. What do you think this means: took them out for an airing?

   5. Who were Tibby's swimming teachers?

   6. Why do you think Tibby was afraid at first?

   7. Why do you think Tibby's mother suddenly dived under the water:
She saw a fish.   She wanted to scare Tibby.   She wanted Tibby to try to swim.   She wanted to hide from her enemies?

   8. What is the meaning of:
a windy March day, the river bank, blind, dived, splashed and struggled, without fear, the wandering otter?

Working with Words

1. Put *a* or *an* in front of these words:

   otter, windy day, eagle, owl, rat.

2. MORE THAN ONE

   We say one brother, two brothers, three brothers.

   Remember: To change from one to MORE THAN ONE, we add S to some words: brother, brothers   cat, cats   tree, trees

   Sometimes we have to add ES, instead of S, to make the new word easier to say: brush, brushes   church, churches

   Remember: When a word ends in SH, CH, S or X, we have to add ES:

   brush, brushes   church, churches   glass, glasses   box, boxes

   Change these words so that they mean MORE THAN ONE:

   dish, match, girl, fox, arch, bush, noise, sister, wish.

3. *Puzzle:* Find a man:

   otter   miner   winter   badger   corner

4. IS and HIS

   Tibby *is* learning to swim.   *His* mother teaches him.

   Remember: HIS means something belongs to HIM.

   Put *is* or *his* into these sentences:

   (i) —— this your kitten?
   (ii) Robert has given a present to —— cousin.
   (iii) This —— your new classroom.

5. *Pairs*

   Tibby's *father and mother*

   Find words which go together, a word from A with one from B, to make four pairs:

A		B
pen, salt, cup, knife	AND	fork, ink, pepper, saucer.

6. *Spelling*

   months: N . . . . . . Dec . . . . . days: Tu . . . . . Wed . . . day
   Will you ple . . . sharpen my brok . . pencil?

7. Sort out these jumbled halves and make sensible sentences:

Penguins	can fly.
Squirrels	are not baby horses.
Ponies	are fierce.
Tigers	live in our woods.
Pigeons	can swim.

8. Which is the biggest: a brook, a river or a stream?

9. Sort out these jumbled words to make sentences and write them properly:

(i) fierce are wolves animals
(ii) can swim I little a

10. Use these words in a sentence: by the river

Find Out

1. Find out what these words mean:

a *poor* man, *Pour* water   there, the, tree, three
a river *bank*, a *Bank* in the High Street
a *March* day, soldiers *march*   *Dear* John, a *dear* coat
I do not *mind*. Please *mind* the baby.
acorn, born, corn, horn, torn, worn

Use one word from each group in sentences of your own.

2. *Dictionary Work*

Find these words in your dictionary, then write down the page-number of each one and the meaning given there:

dab, dairy, daisy, damp, day, dirty, dizzy, doctor, dog, dozen.

3. WILD ANIMALS

Make a list of wild animals which live in our own country, like otters.

4. "Tibby Otter and his three brothers were born on a *windy* March day."

Make these words end in Y, being very careful with their spelling:

rain, snow, frost, ice, sun, dust, gloom, noise, oil, rock.

5

The Moon

The moon has a face like the clock in the hall;
  She shines on thieves on the garden wall,
On streets and fields and harbour quays,
  And birdies asleep in the forks of the trees.

The squalling cat and the squeaking mouse,
  The howling dog by the door of the house,
The bat that lies in bed at noon,
  All love to be out by the light of the moon.

But all of the things that belong to the day
  Cuddle to sleep to be out of the way;
And flowers and children close their eyes
  Till up in the morning the sun shall rise.

Robert Louis Stevenson

Questions about the Poem

A1. Find two round things in the first line of the poem.

2. Find five things on which the moon shines.

3. What are the birds doing?

4. Where is the dog?

5. Find four animals which like to be out at night.

6. Which go to sleep at night:

    bats, flowers, children, the moon?

B1. How does the moon look like a clock?

2. Why do you think thieves are on the garden wall?

3. What is the difference between a table-fork and the fork of a tree?

4. Which are noisy in the poem:

    a cat, a mouse, a dog, a bat or birds?

5. When do bats sleep?

6. When do flowers and children wake up again?

7. Write this sentence, filling in the spaces:

    The moon shines at ——, the —— shines in the day ——.

8. What is the meaning of:

    the hall, thieves, harbour, quays, squalling, squeaking, howling, the bat, cuddle to sleep?

Working with Words

1. Add *s* or *es* to these words to make them mean MORE THAN ONE:

    brush, face, clock, garden, stitch, flower, box, watch.

2. NAMING-WORDS

    "The *moon* has a *face* like the *clock* in the *hall*."

    The words moon, face, clock and hall are the NAMES of things.

    Remember: The names of things are called NAMING-WORDS:

    moon, face, clock, hall, apple, boy, woman, desk, book, school.

    We can put A, AN or THE in front of naming-words and it makes sense:

    the moon, a face, an apple.

    Write down six naming-words.

3. THERE and THEIR

    Sit over *there*.

    Flowers and children close *their* eyes and go to sleep.

    Remember: THERE is a place. It ends in HERE (a place).

    THEIR means something belongs to THEM.
    Both words begin with THE.

    Put *there* or *their* into these sentences:

    (i) I left my library book on that table over ——.
    (ii) The Smith family have just moved into —— new house.
    (iii) —— is your bicycle.

4. *Spelling*

    months: D . . . . Jan . . . .   days: W . . . . Th . . . day

    My fa . . . . was p . . ling the roller on the lawn.

5. ALL ARE WHAT?

    Say what they all are on each line:

    hawk, blackbird, thrush, starling
    oak, chestnut, elm, beech, poplar
    lion, tiger, elephant, bear
    plane, screwdriver, saw, hammer
    pullover, coat, hat, shirt, skirt

6. *Puzzle:* Find a time of day:

    moon   clock   noon   sleep   wrist-watch

7. *Rhymes*

Words which RHYME end in THE SAME SOUND, like ball, fall.

Remember: They do not have to end in the same letters: go, blow; by, lie.

Which words in the poem rhyme with mouse, day, eyes?

8. Choose the right words:

    (i) Our cat likes (to, two, too) go out hunting.

    (ii) (As, Has) your dog been chasing cats again?

    (iii) My uncle (is, his) coming this afternoon.

9. Pick out the words which tell us about MOVING:

    run, shout, jump, crawl, lie, march, stare, snarl, hop, shine.

10. Use these words in a sentence: on the garden wall

Find Out

1. Find out what these words mean:

    a garden, gardening, a gardener   light(2), fight, right(2)

    all, ball, call, fall, hall, stall, tall, wall   bat(2)

    cat, chat, coal, coat, coach, couch   dog, fog, frog, log

Use one word from each group in sentences of your own.

2. *Dictionary Work*

Find these words in your dictionary, then write down the page-number of each one and the meaning given there:

    eagle, early, eel, eight, elbow, elf, empty, enough, evening, eyelash.

3. BIRDS

Make a list of wild birds which live in Britain, like sparrows.

4. "The *squalling* cat and the *squeaking* mouse,
The *howling* dog by the door of the house"

What do we call the NOISES made by these animals and birds:

    a dog (several words), a happy cat, an angry lion, a hen, a donkey,
    a frog, a pig, a horse, a duck, an owl?

6

A Bedtime Game

Edward lived with Aunt Kezia in a house on the hill. On windy nights when the house rocked with the force of the gale, Edward would lie in bed, pretending he was on a ship at sea.

Sometimes he would be shipwrecked, clinging to a spar. He would be cast up on an island, where there were coconut palms, friendly people, and bright-coloured birds in the trees.

The people would give him bananas and milk from the coconut. They would hang a wreath of flowers round his neck, and beg him to stay.

Edward always fell asleep before he could make up his mind whether to stay. When he woke, the sunlight would be streaming into his little room, and Aunt Kezia calling him to come down to his porridge.

From *The Lifeboat Fish* by Dora Broome

Questions about the Story

A 1. (a) What was the boy's name?   (b) What was his aunt's name?

2. Where was his aunt's house?

3. What did Edward do in bed on windy nights?

4. (a) What is a shipwreck?   (b) Is it a real shipwreck in the story?

5. When the people fed Edward, where did the milk come from:

   a cow, a coconut, a milkman's van or a dairy?

6. Did Edward really visit an island?   How do you know?

B 1. Why do you think it was on *windy nights* that he pretended to be on a ship?

2. ". . clinging to a spar" Guess what a *spar* is.

3. Say what you think this means:

   The house rocked.

4. Why do you think Edward thought about *coconut palms* and *bright-coloured* birds?

5. What was the weather like next morning?

6. Why did his aunt shout?

7. How do we know that Edward was not dreaming?

8. What is the meaning of:

   windy nights, gale, pretending, shipwrecked, coconut palms, bananas, make up his mind, sunlight would be streaming, porridge?

Working with Words

1. Pick out all the NAMING-WORDS:

   The boy lived with his aunt in a house on a hill.

2. COMMA

   When we pause to take a breath in a sentence, we put a comma, like this:

   The boy had no brothers, so he had to find friends to play with, or he would have been very lonely.

   If we write a list of things, we put commas, like this:

   I like apples, pears, plums and cherries.
   A large, heavy, iron bar fell off the bench.

   Remember: Do NOT put a comma before the word AND.
   Do NOT put a comma at the *end* of a list, like this:

   A large, heavy, iron, bar fell off the bench. WRONG

   Put commas into these sentences:

   (i) Most children like jam honey syrup and marmalade.
   (ii) In the morning when Edward awoke the sun was shining.
   (iii) A cold little black lamb stood shivering in the snow.

3. Write S if the two words mean the same; D if they are different:

   (1) hill, valley (2) windy, sunny (3) gale, breeze (4) hit, strike
   (5) car, coach (6) gift, present (7) beg, ask (8) asleep, awake

4. *Puzzle:* Find a wind:

   sunshine   hail   rain   gale   snowstorm

5. WHERE and WERE

   Where are you going?
   We *were* working hard.

   Remember: WHERE is a place, like HERE and THERE.

   Put *where* or *were* into these sentences:

   (i) We —— all very tired.
   (ii) The children —— working very hard.
   (iii) I know —— the footballs are kept.

6. *Spelling*

months: J . . . . . . Feb . . . . . days: Th . . . . . . F . . day

The two bab . . . were crying aga . . in their prams.

7. Put *a* or *an* in front of these words:

house, hill, island, coconut, oak-tree, Easter egg, present, arrow.

8. Add *s* or *es* to make these words mean MORE THAN ONE:

house, island, fish, gale, dish, arch.

9. Choose the right words from the brackets:

(i) Will you (to, two, too) boys please go (to, two, too) the shops?
(ii) (As, Has) John come back yet?
(iii) (Is, His) this your book?

10. What do we call (1) the children of kings and queens, (2) their home?

11. Use these words in a sentence: a house on a hill

Find Out

1. Find out what these words mean:

live, love, lovely, lonely, lively   be, bee, been, bean
bill, chill, fill, frill, hill, kill, mill, pill, pillow, still, will, willow
might, night, tight, bright, fright   would, wood

Use one word from each group in sentences.

2. *Dictionary Work*

Find these words in your dictionary, then write down the page-number of each one and the meaning given there:

fairy, family, farmer, feather, fence, fetch, field, firework, fortnight, friend.

3. FRUIT

Make a list of fruit, like bananas and blackberries.

4. Some words can have more than one meaning, like ROCK:

(1) to ROCK a boat   (2) a hard ROCK or stone

Find the DOUBLE MEANINGS of swift, cold, lie, kind, wood, notice, well, dear, bank, fast.

7

The Red-Cap Gnomes

When Nils was twelve years old he was sent up to mind the sheep on Nine Hills, under which the Red-Cap Gnomes mined for silver and gold. All day long the tap-tap of their hammers could be heard, but when night fell they all trooped out to enjoy themselves in the moonlight. And there they danced until the bells on their caps rang and the buckles on their shoes and belts sparkled.

Nils had never seen a Gnome. When he asked Kurt, the Shepherd, about them, the old man said: "Gnomes! You'll never see one unless you were born on a Sunday."

"I WAS born on a Sunday!" cried Nils in delight.

"You're here to look after the sheep," said Kurt; "why, you can't even count your Shepherd's score yet without getting stuck! When I was your age I could say it twenty times over without making a mistake."

And he began to count: "Onetherum, twotherum, cockerum, quetherum, shaterum, wineberry, wigtail, tarrydiddle, Den!"

From *Traditional Tales* by E. Lucia Turnbull

Questions about the Story

A1. Who was twelve?

2. (a) Where did he go?   (b) Why?

3. What did the gnomes or elves do during the daytime?

4. What did they do at night?

5. What was the shepherd's name?

6. How many gnomes had Nils seen?

B1. (a) Who was digging under Nine Hills?   (b) Why?

2. Why did the gnomes' cap-bells ring?

3. (a) Who told Nils that only people born on Sundays could see gnomes?
   (b) What work did this old man do?

4. Why was Nils very pleased?

5. What do you think the Shepherd's score was for?

6. (a) Who hammered?   (b) Who danced?

7. (a) What tinkled?   (b) What shone?

8. What is the meaning of:

   mind the sheep, mined for silver and gold, Red-Cap Gnomes,
   the tap-tap of their hammers,   all trooped out,   buckles, delight,
   without getting stuck?

Working with Words

1. Put capital letters, commas and full stops into these sentences:

   (i) most boys like football cricket running and swimming
   (ii) when they reached the station Peter bought the tickets

2. PARENTS and CHILDREN

   Baby sheep are called LAMBS.

   Which animals or birds are the parents of these young ones:

   calves, puppies, kittens, tadpoles, owlets, ducklings?

3. FOR and FOUR

   What do you like *for* dinner?
   Our cat has *four* kittens.

   Remember: FOUR is the number 4.

   Put *for* or *four* into these sentences:

   (i) We go home from school at —— o'clock.
   (ii) —— soldiers stood at the castle gate.
   (iii) I am tired of waiting —— you.

4. Choose the right words from the ones in the brackets:

   (i) We could (here, hear) a dog howling.
   (ii) (There, Their) were several rats in the barn.
   (iii) (Where, Were) you annoyed when you lost?

5. What are the opposites of these words, like rich, poor:

   old, under, ask, here, with, wrong, never, good, lovely, come?

6. *Puzzle:* Find a day:

   Christmas   Easter   Wednesday   autumn   February

7. Put these words into the sentences: sheep   sleep   steep   sweep

   (i) We cannot —— because of the noisy traffic.
   (ii) Please —— up that broken glass.
   (iii) This hill is very ——.
   (iv) I counted twenty —— in the field.

8. ALL ARE WHAT? Say what they all are on each line:

red, scarlet, crimson, pink
rounders, golf, football, tennis
English, Arithmetic, History, Geography, Mathematics
shepherd, postman, fisherman, engine-driver

9. *Spelling*

months: F . . . . . . Mar . . days: F . . . . . Sat . . . . .
David a . . too m . . y cakes at the party.

10. Use these words in a sentence: twelve years old

Find Out

1. Find out what these words mean:

Which kind? A wicked *witch* heard, a herd
bent, dent, lent, rent, sent, scent, tent, went, m*ea*nt
caps, capes, scraps, scrapes ring(2), rung(2)

Use one word from each group in sentences.

2. *Dictionary Work*

Find these words in your dictionary, then write down the page-number
of each one and the meaning given there:

gaily, gale, gallon, gallop, gamble, garage, giant, glove,
greengrocer, grocer.

3. TOOLS AND OTHER THINGS USED AT WORK

Give each worker in List A something from List B which he uses at work:

List A: carpenter, train guard, farmer, postman, bus conductor,
gardener
List B: bag, green flag, spade, plough, tickets, saw

4. The gnomes came out at night to *enjoy* themselves.

Which of these words tell us about being HAPPY:

sad, glad, hate, unhappy, frown, quarrel, fight, pleased, smile,
cry, laugh, weep, kind, cruel, fierce, friendly?

8

Left All Alone

Once upon a time in the Land of Long Ago there was a Little Brown Bird, and he was very unhappy because he had broken his wing.

That was bad enough. He did not like to have to go hop, hop, hop until his wing got well, instead of flying through the air.

Worse still, winter was coming. Soon the North Wind would go roaring through the woods, shaking the leaves from the trees, bringing the snow, and covering the blue sky with grey clouds.

All the Little Brown Bird's friends were saying, "Winter is coming. Winter is coming. We must go, go, go."

What would the poor Little Brown Bird do without them?

Each day some of them spread their wings and flew away to warm countries where the sun shone, and there were leaves on the trees and flowers in the grass, and plenty of food for little birds to eat all through the winter.

Every day more and more went, till at last the Little Brown Bird was left all alone, and he was very unhappy indeed.

From *The Little Brown Bird* by Elizabeth Clark

Questions about the Story

A 1. Was the bird sad or merry?

2. Why did he feel like that?

3. What was coming?

4. What would soon roar:

      a lion, the wind, a tiger, winter?

5. What did the bird's friends do?

6. Why did they leave the Little Brown Bird behind?

B 1. Why did the bird have to hop when it wanted to move about?

2. What was worse than having to hop all the time?

3. (a) Where did the other birds go? (b) Why?

4. Why did the leaves fall off the trees?

5. If you were the Little Brown Bird left all alone, what would you do?

6. Why would the clouds be grey, not white?

7. How do you think the bird's wing was broken?

8. What is the meaning of:

      the Land of Long Ago, go hop, hop, hop, roaring through the
woods, warm countries, plenty of food, left all alone?

Working with Words

1. What are nestlings: baby (frogs, birds, geese, mice, rabbits)?
   What do we call the babies of ducks, fowls, bears, foxes?

2. MORE THAN ONE

   In Exercise 4 we saw that we can add s or es to some words to make them mean MORE THAN ONE:

   bird, birds bush, bushes

   Sometimes we do not add s or es. If a word ends in F or FE, like leaf or wife, we usually change the F or FE to V and add ES:

   leaf, leaves wife, wives

   Make these words mean MORE THAN ONE:

   wolf, calf, half, loaf, knife, thief.

3. BLEW and BLUE

   The North Wind *blew* the leaves off the trees.
   There were no clouds in the *blue* sky.

   Remember: BLUE is a colour BLEW tells us about BLOWING.

   Put *blue* or *blew* into these sentences:

   (i) Janet has a new —— dress.
   (ii) The wind —— the balloon over the rooftops.
   (iii) I counted five —— cars in the car-park.

4. *Spelling*

   months: M . . . . Ap . . .   days: S . . . . S . . . . .
   This is the big . . . . piece and that is the sma . . . . . piece.

5. Choose the right words:

   (i) (Where, Were) is your teacher?
   (ii) The children found (there, their) Christmas presents by (there, their) beds.
   (iii) Come (here, hear, ear), you naughty dog!

6. Pick out all the naming-words:

   a bird, unhappy, broken, wing, the wind, roaring, woods, leaf.

7. *Puzzle:* Find a happy word:

    sad   crying   glad   howling   screaming

8. Write two short sentences, putting *hopping* in one and *hoping* in the other.

9. What are the missing words?

    one, ——, three, four, five
    spring, summer, autumn, ——
    January, ——, March, April
    Monday, ——, ——, Thursday, Friday

10. What are the opposites of:

    a *kind* master, *under* the bridge, *dirty* hands, come, question, early?

11. Use these words in a sentence: left all alone

Find Out

1. Find out what these words mean:

    roar, roam, road, rode, rowed, roast   some, sum, sun, son
    cow, how, low(2), mow, now, tow
    bow, row, sow (two ways of saying each one)

Use two words from each group in sentences.

2. *Dictionary Work*

Find these words in your dictionary, then write down the page-number of each one and the meaning given there:

    hammer, handkerchief, happy, hawk, heap, hedge, herd, herring, hoof, hurry.

3. NORTH, SOUTH, EAST and WEST

Try to think of three things for each word, like *North* and *South* America OR words which have North, South, East or West in them, like Northampton and Southend.

4. The Little Brown Bird was very unhappy because its wing was broken. Which of these words tell us about being UNHAPPY:

    weep, jolly, sad, happy, tears, gay, merry, crying, glad, laughing, welcome, pleasant, miserable, scowling, accident, illness, cheer?

The Girl and the Skylark

Once upon a time there was a little girl who sang very prettily. "Tra-la-la," she went, "tra-la-la." And everyone said: "My oh my, she sings like a skylark."

Wherever she went, the little girl only opened her mouth, only let the breath come gently out with a song, and everyone said: "What a wonder she is, the little lark!"

So one day the little girl went into a field to show the skylarks. "I'll show them," she thought, "I'll show the skylarks I can sing quite as well as they can. Everyone says so. So that's how it must be."

Very soon she saw a skylark, a dull brown bird and not at all gay. The little girl smoothed out her blue-and-yellow frock, and patted her golden hair. "My goodness!" she thought, "HE doesn't look important."

The skylark walked along the ground, then he ran a little way. "Why, he doesn't even hop," thought the little girl. "What a VERY dull bird he is indeed." And she cleared her throat, getting ready to sing.

Suddenly the lark leaped into the air. Beating his strong wings, up he flew, head to the wind. And he sang! How he sang!

From *The Skylark* by Leila Berg

Questions about the Story

A 1. What could the girl do very well?

2. She sang like a (parrot, canary, lark, thrush). Which?

3. What was she going to show the skylarks?

4. What was dull and did not look important?

5. (a) What was like gold?   (b) What had two colours?

6. What did the skylark do, after walking and running?

B 1. Why did people call the little girl "the little lark"?

2. Why did she go out into the field, one day?

3. Why did she think that she was a good singer?

4. Why do you think she expected skylarks to look gay and important?

5. Why do you think the girl smoothed out her frock and patted her hair?

6. "And she cleared her throat, getting ready to sing."
   How would she do this?   Why?

7. "And he sang! How he sang!"
   Put a word into the space:

   "And he sang! How —— he sang!"

8. What is the meaning of:

   Once upon a time, sang very prettily, Tra-la-la, let the breath come gently out, What a wonder she is, smoothed out, important, a very dull bird, leaped into the air, head to the wind?

Working with Words

1. Make these words mean MORE THAN ONE:

   shelf, calf, leaf, knife, thief, wolf.

2. MORE ABOUT CAPITAL LETTERS

   Our own names must begin with a CAPITAL LETTER:

   (i) Family names or surnames: Smith, Brown, Jones, Robinson
   (ii) Christian names (forenames): John, Margaret, Sally, Derek

   I (myself) is always a capital letter: Please may I come with you?

   Write these sentences properly:

   (i) a little girl named susan brown fell off the swing
   (ii) may john and i come with you, please?
   (iii) two boys were waiting for roger jackson

3. BE and BEE

   You will *be* late.

   A *bee* stung me on the leg.

   Remember: A BEE stings.

   Put *be* or *bee* into these sentences:

   (i) Do you think you will —— long?
   (ii) The —— kept flying round my head.
   (iii) You must —— brave and stop yelling.

4. *Puzzle:* Find a dull word:

   bright   shining   glossy   dark   gay

5. everybody   jump   sly   gap   swift   neat

   Which word means the same as (1) quick   (2) everyone   (3) cunning
   (4) leap   (5) tidy   (6) space?

6. Pick out first of all three SOFT things, then three HARD things:

   little, rock, handkerchief, mountain, story, fur, happy, brick,
   cotton-wool, sky, rich.

7. Sort out these jumbled words to make proper sentences:

   (i) sing skylarks sweetly can very
   (ii) the lesson what next is?

8. *Spelling*

months: A . . . . M . . days: S . . . . W . . . .

We saw bu . . . . cups, dais . . . and dand . . . . . in the field.

9. Which is the biggest: a skylark, an eagle, a robin or a duck?

Which is the smallest: a cottage, a room, a cupboard or a bungalow?

10. Choose the right words:

(i) Would you like (to, two, too) go now?

(ii) (To, Two, Too) little kittens are hiding in the corner.

(iii) Ian (as, has) no money left.

(iv) Our dog (is, his) very friendly.

11. Use these words in a sentence: Once upon a time

Find Out

1. Find out what these words mean:

to *show*, a Flower *Show*   *quite* right, very *quiet*

quite *well*, a deep *well*   I can, a can, candle, cannon

so, sow, sew   hoping, hopping

bay, clay, day, gay, hay, jay, lay, may, pay, ray, say, tray, way

Use one word from each group in sentences of your own.

2. *Dictionary Work*

Find these words in your dictionary, then write down the page-number of each one and the meaning given there:

icicle, idle, impatient, impossible, inch, indoors, infant, insect, invite, island.

3. COLOURS

"The little girl smoothed out her *blue*-and-*yellow* frock, and patted her *golden* hair."

Think of something for each of these colours:

red, white, blue, black, green, yellow, brown, purple, orange.

4. "And everyone *said* . . ."

How do we SPEAK when we do this:

shout, argue, mutter, yell, ask, complain, growl, grumble?

Winter Song

Rain and wind, and wind and rain.
Will the Summer come again?
Rain on houses, on the street,
Wetting all the people's feet.
Though they run with might and main,
Rain and wind, and wind and rain.

Snow and sleet, and sleet and snow.
Will the Winter never go?
What do beggar children do
With no fire to cuddle to,
P'raps with nowhere warm to go?
Snow and sleet, and sleet and snow.

Hail and ice, and ice and hail,
Water frozen in the pail.
See the robins brown and red,
They are waiting to be fed,
Poor dears, battling in the gale,
Hail and ice, and ice and hail.

Katherine Mansfield

Questions about the Poem

A 1. Where does the rain fall?

  2. What does the rain do which is very unpleasant?

  3. Who run hard?

  4. How is Winter cruel to very poor children?

  5. What is there in a bucket:

     milk, ice, ice-cream, oats or wheat?

  6. What are hungry?

B 1. Find in this poem six kinds of wintry weather.

  2. What are the four seasons of the year?

  3. Why are the people running as fast as they can?

  4. How many questions are asked in this poem?

  5. What are beggar children?

  6. Why are the robins called "Poor dears"?

  7. How can robins battle (fight) in a gale? NOT fighting one another.

  8. What is the meaning of:

     run with might and main (run with all their might), sleet, hail, beggar, cuddle to, P'raps, the pail, Winter Song?

Working with Words

1. Write correctly:
    (i) i wish i knew the answer.
    (ii) i think shirley knows the answer.
    (iii) ask peter smith.

2. STILL MORE ABOUT CAPITAL LETTERS

   In Exercise 1 we saw that a sentence must begin with a capital letter. In Exercise 9 we saw that Christian names and surnames begin with a capital letter; also that *I* is always a capital letter.

Our Christian names and surnames are SPECIAL names. All SPECIAL names begin with a CAPITAL LETTER: names of the days of the week, the months of the year, towns, counties, countries, rivers and mountains:

Sunday, December, London, Middlesex, England, River Thames, Mount Everest.

Find which of these names are *special names* and begin them with a capital letter:

rain, wind, manchester, peter, river trent, rivers, jones, tuesday, april, mary, ice, wednesday, ships, lancashire, mountain.

3. *Puzzle:* Find a bird:

rain   wind   swallow   sleet   hail   gale

4. Which is the biggest: a mouse, cat, kitten or rat?

Which is the smallest: a blade of grass, a field, a meadow or a lawn?

5. NO, KNOW and NOW

No, you may not go!
Do you *know* the answer?
You may come in *now.*

Remember: The longest word, KNOW, means KNOWING something.

Put *no, know* or *now* into these sentences:

(i) Do you —— the way?
(ii) ——, I don't —— the way.
(iii) —— we are lost!

6. *Spelling*

months: M . . J . . e   lessons: . . glish   Corr . . . .
I   mis . . .   the post.   We played in the   f . . lds   today.

7. *Rhymes*

Which words in the poem rhyme with   rain, feet, red?

8. Say WIND in two different ways, then use the two words, writing two sentences.

9. Write s if the two words mean the same; d if they are different:

(1) summer, autumn (2) rain, mountain (3) pail, bucket (4) big, large (5) robin, wren (6) red, blue (7) gale, storm.

10. Change these words to mean MORE THAN ONE:

street, fire, coat, scarf, lamb, calf, fox, knife, match, leaf.

11. Use these words in a sentence: in the gale

Find Out

1. Find out what these words mean:

gain, main, pain, rain, stain, train, vain(2), a pain, a window-pane pouring with *rain*, reins, the king's *reign*   street, straight sleet, sleep, sleeve   the *main* door, a lion's *mane*

Use one word from each group in sentences.

2. *Dictionary Work*

Find these words in your dictionary, then write down the page-number of each one and the meaning given there:

jack, jay, jealous, jingle, jockey, joke, juice, jumble, jump, jungle.

3. SEASONS

spring, summer, autumn and winter.
Make lists of things which we find in each season, like this:

spring: daffodils, lambs, . . .

4. What are these PAIRS, like cup and saucer:

—— and comb, —— and fork, —— and pepper, —— and fire, pen and ——, —— and butter, snow and ——, husband and ——, —— and aunt, —— and mother, son and ——, king and ——?

Do you know any more pairs?

11

Fifty Red Caps

Once upon a time, there was a man who had fifty red night-caps to sell at a fair. His wife put them into a great bag for him which he carried over his shoulder.

It was a very hot country and presently the man's way lay through a wood, so, when he came to the shade, he put down his bag and sat down to rest, and soon he took one of the red night-caps out of his bag, put it on, lay down and went to sleep.

Now there were monkeys in that wood, and by and by a great old ape came stealing down out of the trees, seized one of the red night-caps out of the bag, popped it on his head, and ran up into a tree and sat there grinning and chattering. By and by another ape came stealing down and he too took a red night-cap, put it on and ran up into the tree and he too sat in the tree grinning and chattering. Then another ape took another red night-cap, and then another, until at last there were forty-nine monkeys in forty-nine red night-caps, sitting in the trees chattering and calling out.

From *Fairy Tales from the British Isles* by Amabel Williams-Ellis

Questions about the Story

A 1. What was the man going to sell?

2. Where did his wife put them?

3. How was the bag carried?

4. On the way to the fair, the man went through a (river, wood, town, park). Which?

5. Which animals were up in the trees?

6. How do we know that they were mischievous and liked to play tricks?

B 1. Why did the man sit down?

2. What did he do just before he lay down?

3. Finish this:

   The first cap was stolen by ——.

4. How do you think the monkeys knew how to wear the caps?

5. Why do you think they were chattering and calling out?

6. What do you think the man would say when he awoke?

7. How do we know that this did not happen in our country?

8. Say what these words mean:

   night-caps, a fair, presently, the man's way, the shade, a great old ape, came stealing down, seized, grinning and chattering.

Working with Words

1. Which of these words should begin with a capital letter:

   thursday, blackbird, february, ceiling, marilyn, scotland?

2. DESCRIBING-WORDS

   In the story, the night-caps were RED; RED tells us more about the caps. It tells us what they were like. It DESCRIBES them.

   Find in the story the DESCRIBING-WORDS which tell us more about a bag, a country and an ape.

49

We can put describing-words with other words in the story, like this:

a fair: a busy fair, a noisy fair, an exciting fair.

Think of describing-words to put with these words in the story:

a —— wood, —— monkeys, his —— head, a —— tree

3. *Noises*

What *things* (NOT people, animals or birds) make these noises:

tinkle, jingle, slam, rustle, squeak, rattle, creak, crash, bang, hiss?

4. Choose the right words:

(i) Come at (for, four) o'clock (for, four) your library book.

(ii) The rough wind (blue, blew) away the (blue, blew) balloon.

5. *Puzzle:* Find a colour:

fifty   scarlet   circus   reading   ape

6. Put capital letters and full stops in these sentences:

(i) the man went to the fair

(ii) his name was john smith

7. ALL ARE WHAT?

Say what they all are on each line:

swallow, robin, canary, sparrow
oak, ash, elm, willow, fir
man, woman, boy, girl
England, Scotland, Wales, Ireland
bang, crash, clatter, boom

8. *Spelling*

months: J . . . and J . . .   seasons: spr . . . su . . . .

I was lonely   unt . .   my best   fr . . nd   came.

9. BY and BUY

By the side of the river we found a big nest.

I am going to *buy* my mother a birthday present.

Remember: BUY is BUYING things with money.

Put *by* or *buy* into these sentences:

    (i) We were beaten —— a good team.

    (ii) It will soon be time to —— Christmas presents.

    (iii) Be careful —— the edge of the lake.

10. If the two words mean the same, write S; if they do not, write N:

    (a) sell, buy (b) great, huge (c) hot, icy (d) out, in (e) came, went (f) seize, grab (g) rap, wrap (h) angry, furious

11. Use these words in a sentence: through a wood

Find Out

1. Find out what these words mean:

    a fair, bus-fare, fair hair, not fair (unfair)   steal, steel

    red caps, I have *read* it.   great, a grate

    air, bare, bear, care, dare, glare, hair, hare, lair, mare, pair, pear, pare, rare, stare, tear(2), wear   through, threw

Use one word from each group in sentences.

2. *Dictionary Work*

Find these words in your dictionary, then write down the page-number of each one and the meaning given there:

    keen, keg, kennel, kettle, kid, kitchen, knee, knife, knock, knot.

3. ANIMALS

Think of six animals which can climb trees and six which cannot.

4. "... a great old ape ... *seized* one of the red night-caps ..."

HAND ACTIONS

What do we do when we fling, grab, grasp, hit, hold, hurl, knock, nip, pat, press, pull, push, rap, snatch, squash, squeeze, stroke, tap, throw, touch?

12

Market-Day

Ivy was happy in the market. She walked round and round the stalls, looking at all the things. Sometimes a snowflake fell on her head, but she shook it off. Sometimes one stuck to her cheek, but she put out her tongue and licked it away.

She bought a bag of chestnuts from the chestnut man. They were hot in her hands and she ate them one by one. She had a cup of tea from a tea stall on wheels, and from a sweet stall she bought a toffee apple.

When her legs grew tired she sat down on a step and wrapped the ends of her coat round her knees. When she was cold she started to walk again.

Soon lights were lit all along the stalls. They looked like stars. The crowd grew thicker. People laughed and stamped in the snow to keep their feet warm. Ivy stamped too.

The stall-keepers shouted and called for people to come and buy. Ivy bought a pink balloon.

From *The Story of Holly and Ivy* by Rumer Godden

Questions about the Story

A 1. What was the name of the girl who was looking round the market?

2. Describe the weather.

3. What did the girl lick:

an ice-cream, snowflakes, nothing?

4. Why do you think she did such a thing?

5. (a) What did she eat? (b) What did she drink?

6. What did she do when she felt tired?

B 1. Why do you think Ivy was happy?

2. Did this happen in spring, summer, autumn or winter?

3. Was it morning, midday, afternoon, evening or midnight?

4. Was it still snowing? How do you know?

5. Make a list of everything which Ivy bought.

6. What did she do to keep warm? Give two answers.

7. What twinkled?

8. What is the meaning of:

market, stalls, snowflake, chestnuts, toffee apple, The crowd grew thicker, stall-keepers?

Working with Words

1. Pick out the describing-words:
    - (i) Ivy was happy in the market.
    - (ii) She bought a pink balloon.
    - (iii) I found a long, heavy, black, iron bar.

2. PEOPLE'S WORK

    "The *stall-keepers* shouted and called for people to come and buy."
    What do we call the people who do these jobs:
    - (a) look after people who are ill   (b) bring our letters
    - (c) own farms   (d) build houses   (e) clean and look after schools
    - (f) collect our rubbish   (g) dig for coal   (h) catch fish
    - (i) sell toothpaste, medicines and soap   (j) take bus-fares?

3. *Puzzle:* Find a girl's name:

    Malcolm   Oxford   Surrey   Shirley   China

4. *Spelling*

    months: . . . y   Au . . . .   seasons: su . . . .   au . . . .
    What a   hi . .   mount . . .   we must climb!
    My   clo . . . .   are soaking wet.

5. "The *crowd* grew thicker." What are these groups of people:
    spectators, a queue, a team, an army, a band(2)?

6. OF and OFF

    She took her necklace out *of* the drawer.
    The boy fell *off* the slide.
    Remember: out OF, a piece OF cake
    OFF the table: Do NOT say OFF OF the table

    Put *of* or *off* into these spaces:
    - (a) a cup —— tea   (b) the edge —— the pond   (c) go —— in a hurry
    - (d) a bag —— money   (e) take —— your cap   (f) fell out —— the sky

7. Pick out the right word in the brackets:
    - (i) I (saw, seen) him break the fence.
    - (ii) He said I (done, did) it.
    - (iii) We (no, know, now) your name.

8. Sort out these halves to make proper sentences:

John and Elizabeth   build nests.
Birds   have four legs and are very strong.
Wild rabbits   are cousins.
Donkeys   live in holes in the ground.

9. Write three short sentences, using these words, one in each sentence:

stars   stares   stairs

10. Which of these has most trees: a wood, a forest, a small orchard?

11. Use these words in a sentence: round and round

Find Out

1. Find out what these words mean:

Ivy sitting on a wall, *ivy* growing on a wall   one, won
licked it, liked it, locked it   eat, ate
She *bought* some chestnuts. She *brought* some chestnuts.   warm, warn
Stamp hard. A threepenny *stamp*.   rap, wrap

Use one word from each group in sentences.

2. *Dictionary Work*

Find these words in your dictionary, then write down the page-number of each one and the meaning given there:

ladder, lake, lamb, lame, laugh, leaf, learn, library, loaf, lucky.

3. PARTS OF THE BODY

Find seven parts of the body in the Market-Day story.
What are these parts of the body:

two e . . . and two e . . .   one n . . . and one n . . .   two l . . . and
two l . . .   eight f . . . . . and two t . . . . .   ten t . . .?

4. "The stall-keepers *shouted* . . ."

How do we SPEAK when we do this:

order, groan, moan, sigh, sob, gabble, mumble, whisper?

13

The Old Man and His Wife

An old man and an old woman lived in a little wooden house. All round the house there was a garden, crammed with flowers, and potatoes, and beetroots, and cabbages. And in one corner of the house there was a narrow wooden stairway which went up and up, twisting and twisting, into a high tower. In the top of the tower was a dovecot, and on the top of the dovecot was a flat roof.

Now, the old woman was never content with the doings of the old man. She scolded all day, and she scolded all night. If there was too much rain, it was the old man's fault; and if there was a drought, and all green things were parched for lack of water, well, the old man was to blame for not altering the weather. And though he was old and tired, it was all the same to her how much work she put on his shoulders. The garden was full. There was no room in it at all, not even for a single pea. And all of a sudden the old woman sets her heart on growing turnips.

"But there is no room in the garden," says the old man.

"Sow them on the top of the dovecot," says the old woman.

"But there is no earth there."

"Carry earth up and put it there," says she.

So the old man laboured up and down with his tired old bones, and covered the top of the dovecot with good black earth.

From *Old Peter's Russian Tales* by Arthur Ransome

56

Questions about the Story

A1. Where did the two old people live?

2. Where was their garden:

   in front of the house, behind it, at the side or right round it?

3. The old woman was (kind, hard-working, spiteful, silent). Which?

4. What did she suddenly want?

5. What did her husband say about this?

6. Where did she want to have an extra garden?

B1. What does the word CRAMMED tell us about the garden?

2. (a) Where was the tower? (b) What was it, really?

3. What kind of stairs were in the tower?

4. A dove is like a (rook, pigeon, owl, parrot). Which?

5. Which two sentences tell us that the garden was full?

6. What silly task did the old woman order her husband to do?

7. Describe these vegetables:

   potatoes, beetroots, cabbages.

8. What is the meaning of:

   a narrow wooden stairway, a high tower, a dovecot, never content, scolded, the old man's fault, parched, his tired old bones, a drought, laboured?

Working with Words

1. What kind of work do these people do:

   fireman, ploughman, actor, doctor, tailor, fisherman?

   What is the difference between an actor and an actress?

2. DOING-WORDS

   Words which say that we DO something are called DOING-WORDS, like these: he SAYS, they RUN, I HIT, the birds FLEW.

When we are doing something NOW, like running, we can say:

I run, we run, you run, they run   he runs, she runs, it runs

OR: I *am* running; he (or she or it) *is* running; we (or you or they) *are* running

Remember: Adding ING: 1. If the doing-word ends in E, we usually leave out the E: come, coming love, loving give, giving care, caring

2. Many words have DOUBLE LETTERS before ING: run, running stop, stopping begin, beginning

Choose the right words in the brackets:

(i) You (am, is, are) late again.

(ii) Carol (talks, talk) too much in class.

(iii) The rabbit (run, runs) quickly when the fox (come, comes).

Add ING to these doing-words: run, go, come, race, hit

3. *Spelling*

months: A . . . . . S . . . . seasons: a . . . . . w . . . . .
Stop cli . . . . . up the tree! Answer my que . . . . . quickly!

4. Find four describing-words in the last sentence of the story about the old man and his wife; then use two of them in a sentence of your own.

5. Write these sentences correctly:

(i) a blackbird was sitting on our garden fence

(ii) we went home at seven o'clock

6. WEAK and WEEK

Elephants are strong, not *weak*. Come again next *week*.

Remember: WEEK is TIME

Put *weak* or *week* into these sentences:

(i) There are seven days in a ——.

(ii) I felt very —— after my long illness.

(iii) You will feel —— for another ——.

7. *Puzzle:* Find a vegetable:

flowers   cauliflower   mole   stork   catkins

8. Put the boys and men into one list and the girls and women into another:

uncle, aunt   mother, father   nephew, niece   queen, king
son, daughter

9. satisfied   soil   small   changing   weary   set

Which words mean the same as these words:

(a) tired   (b) content   (c) earth   (d) little   (e) altering   (f) sow?

10. Use in a sentence: An old man and an old woman

Find Out

1. Find out what these words mean:

wooden, woollen   tap(2), tip(2), top(2)   roofs, hoofs
fright, light(2), might(2), night, right(2), sight, slight
tired, tried   a *flat* roof, a flat

Use one word from each group in sentences.

2. *Dictionary Work*

Find these words in your dictionary, then write down the page-number of each one and the meaning given there:

magpie, mallet, mare, marmalade, match, merry, mile, minute, monkey, mushroom.

3. VEGETABLES

Make a list of vegetables, like potatoes, beetroots and cabbages.

4. "She *scolded* all day, and she *scolded* all night."

Which of these are UNKIND or BAD ACTIONS:

stealing, obeying, scowling, fighting, helping, sulking, hitting someone, lying (telling lies), curing, behaving, misbehaving?

14

A Young Rabbit's Adventures

From behind a tuft of heather on the moor, a young rabbit peeped out. He had wandered away from his mother, and was out to see the world for himself. Mother was busy nibbling the bark from a young tree, but the young rabbit did not want to eat. He wanted to enjoy life.

How lovely the moor was on that sunny day! Birds sang, butterflies flitted by, and all seemed gay. Bees buzzed amongst the heather, and insects were on the wing.

Just as our young rabbit was wondering where to go next, he saw a strange sight. A small, curious animal was coming, and it was doing all sorts of funny tricks. Look! it was standing on its hind legs. Now it was turning head over heels. How exciting this was, to be sure! It was even better than the circus. Never had the rabbit seen such antics. He really must scurry off, and tell his mother. So off he bolted, like the wind.

"Mother! Mother!" he gasped, as he reached her side. "Come and look! Come and look! There's a little brown animal walking upside down!"

From *Our Wondrous World* by P. A. Barons

Questions about the Story

A 1. What was the young rabbit sitting behind?

2. What was his mother doing?

3. What was the weather like:

    cold, frosty, sunny or wet?

4. What were the birds doing?

5. Why did the young rabbit run to his mother:

    He was afraid. It was dinnertime. He wanted to tell her what he had seen. She called him back?

6. Did he run fast, very fast, slowly or very slowly?

B 1. Why had the young rabbit left his mother?

2. What do rabbits like to eat (in this story)?

3. What do you think the buzzing bees were doing?

4. Insects were (swarming on the wings of an aeroplane, flying about, nibbling the bark of trees, singing). Which?

5. What strange sight did the young rabbit see?

6. Who does tricks like the little brown animal:

    a wild elephant, a circus clown, a horse or a butterfly?

7. The little brown animal was a fierce weasel which does tricks to try to catch silly young rabbits for dinner. What do you think Mother Rabbit said to her son when he told her what he had seen?

8. What is the meaning of:

    a tuft of heather, the moor, wandered away, to see the world, busy, nibbling, flitted by, a strange sight, *curious* animal, scurry off?

Working with Words

1. Add ING to these doing-words:

    run, drop, live, chase, hop, skip, fall, go.

2. MORE THAN ONE

"Birds sang, *butterflies* flitted by, and all seemed gay."

We saw in Exercise 4 that we add S or ES to some words to make them mean MORE THAN ONE:

bird, birds   thrush, thrushes.

In Exercise 8 we saw that we change some endings from F or FE to VES:

leaf, leaves   wife, wives.

Now we must learn about words which end in Y, like butterfly, fairy, day, boy. There are two things to remember:

(1) If the word ends in AY, EY, OY, UY (a VOWEL before the Y) we add S:

day, days   key, keys   boy, boys   guy, guys

(2) If there is NO VOWEL before the Y we change the Y to I and add ES:

fly, flies   butterfly, butterflies   fairy, fairies   lady, ladies

Make these words mean MORE THAN ONE:

penny, cherry, valley, monkey, army, chimney, donkey, baby.

3. *Puzzle:* Find an insect: magpie, gnat, rabbit, weasel, toad.

4. NEW and KNEW

We have a *new* teacher.

The mother rabbit *knew* that the animal was dangerous.

Remember: KNEW tells us about KNOWING.

Put *new* or *knew* into these sentences:

(i) The conjuror —— all kinds of tricks.
(ii) Caroline's father has bought a —— car.
(iii) I —— you wanted a —— writing-book.

5. Whose homes are these:

kennel, stable, sty, hutch, burrow or warren, house, palace?

6. *Spelling*

months: J . . . . . . F . . . .   lessons: Geog . . . . . Hist . . .
The king sat on his   thr . . .   and   wel . . . ed   the guests.

7. Put a describing-word with each naming-word:

   Describing-words   *Naming-words*

   kind, fierce, cold, deep, hard : river, tiger, keeper, weather, rocks

8. Choose the right words:

   (i) You must (by, buy) the sweets yourself.
   (ii) (Be, Bee) like the busy (be, bee) and work hard.

9. Which words mean MOVING SLOWLY:

   race, charge, trickle, gallop, scamper, rush, crawl, dawdle, stroll?

10. Write this sentence correctly:

   brian green lives in leeds in yorkshire

11. Use these words in a sentence: head over heels

Find Out

1. Find out what these words mean:

   wander, wonder   moor, *more* bread   tree-bark, a dog's bark
   lovely, lonely, lively   see, sea   I *saw* him. I can *saw* it.
   head over *heels*, Ointment *heals* cuts.   bolted(2)

   Use one word from each group in sentences.

2. *Dictionary Work*

   Find these words in your dictionary, then write down the page-number of each one and the meaning given there:

   nail, name, nap, navy, needle, neigh, nest, news, niece, nut.

3. YOUNG ONES

   What special name do we give to the young of these animals or birds:

   cats, dogs, eagles, sheep, horses, deer, geese, ducks, fowls, pigs, goats, swans?

   How many animals have young CUBS?   Name them.

4. Which of these are KIND or GOOD ACTIONS:

   helping, giving, striking, smiling, punching, robbing, killing, hurting, nursing, sharing, cheating, blaming, boasting, annoying?

15

Choosing Their Names

Our old cat has kittens three—
What do you think their names should be?

One is a tabby with emerald eyes,
   And a tail that's long and slender,
And into a temper she quickly flies
   If you ever by chance offend her.
      I think we shall call her this—
      I think we shall call her that—
Now, don't you think that Pepperpot
   Is a nice name for a cat?

One is black, with a frill of white,
   And her feet are all white fur, too;
If you stroke her she carries her tail upright
   And quickly begins to purr, too!
      I think we shall call her this—
      I think we shall call her that—
Now, don't you think that Sootikin
   Is a nice name for a cat?

One is a tortoiseshell, yellow and black,
   With plenty of white about him;
If you tease him, at once he sets up his back,
   He's a quarrelsome one, ne'er doubt him.
      I think we shall call him this—
      I think we shall call him that—
Now, don't you think that Scratchaway
   Is a nice name for a cat?

Thomas Hood

Questions about the Poem

A 1. Which animals are having their names chosen:

old cats, kittens, puppies or cubs?

2. How many of the animals are there?

3. The first one is (fat, bad-tempered, kind, yellow, white). Which?

4. The second one is (black and white, fierce, naughty, old). Which?

5. The third one is (blue, lame, always quarrelling, kind). Which?

6. Where do you think Sootikin's white frill is?

B 1. Which kitten has green eyes?

2. Why should the tabby one be called Pepperpot?

3. Why should the black and white one be called Sootikin?

4. Why should the yellow and black one be called Scratchaway?

5. From clues in the third verse, *tortoiseshell* must be a kind of colour.
   (a) What colour is it?   (b) Why do you think that colour has such a name?

6. Which kitten do you think would make the best pet? Why?

7. Which kittens are BOY-kittens and which are GIRL-kittens? What tells you in the poem?

8. What is the meaning of:

a tabby, long and slender, a temper, offend her, upright, purr, tease him, sets up his back?

Working with Words

1. Make these words mean MORE THAN ONE:

   baby, boy, story, fly, chimney, day.

2. QUESTIONS

   When we write a question, we put a QUESTION MARK at the end, like this: Now, don't you think that Pepperpot is a nice name for a cat?

   Remember: These words can ask questions:

   WHO   WHEN   HOW   WHAT   WHERE   WHY   WHICH

   Who broke the plate? *When* did you break it? *How* did you break it? *What* is the time? *Where* are you going? *Why?* *Which* is the way?

   Write three short questions, using *how* in the first, *when* in the second and *who* in the third. Do not forget the question mark at the end.

3. *Puzzle:* Find a young animal: cat   horse   foal   hare   fox

4. OUR, HOUR and ARE

   Our cat is ten years old.
   I shall be ready in an *hour*.
   Are you ready?

   Remember: HOUR is TIME: Hours, minutes and seconds.
   OUR means something belongs to US.

   Put *our, hour* or *are* into these sentences:

   (i) —— visitors arrived an —— ago.
   (ii) —— you coming to see —— new baby?

5. A or AN

   When a word begins with a SILENT H we put AN in front, not A:

   an hour, an honest man.

   Put *a* or *an* in front of these words:

   hospital, holly-bush, hurry, in —— hour and —— half, hawk.

6. *Spelling*

   colours: w . . . .   bl . .   bl . . .   br . . .   or . . . .   pur . . .
   Tom . . . ow   mor . . . .   we are go . . .   to the seaside.

7. Choose the right words:
    (i) I met (two, to, too) children walking with (there, their) father.
    (ii) (Hear, Ear, Here) is Jean's coat.
    (iii) Six rabbits (were, where) racing across the field.
    (iv) You (for, four) children are making (to, two, too) much noise.

8. *Rhymes*
   Which words in the poem rhyme with three, eyes and black?

9. Think of the opposites of these words:
    happy, hot, high, fat, narrow, long, rich, dark, heavy, last.

10. snow   soot   grass   lion   ice   rose   berry
    Use these words to finish these little sayings:
    as black as —— as brave as a —— as red as a —— as cold as ——
    as green as —— as white as —— as brown as a ——

11. Use in a sentence: our old cat

Find Out

1. Find out what these words mean:
    bell, cell, dell, fell, sell, tell, well(2), yell   fur, fir
    at the *back*, on his *back*, go *back*   cat, cot, cut
    yellow, bellow   right, write   a long *tale*, a long *tail*
    Use one word from each group in sentences.

2. *Dictionary Work*
   Find these words in your dictionary, then write down the page-number
   of each one and the meaning given there:
    ocean, o'clock, ointment, onion, opposite, orange, orchard, otter,
    outlaw, oval.

3. WILD CATS
   Make a list of animals in the wild cat family, like lion and lioness.

4. (a) a nice book   (b) a nice day   (c) a nice old man   (d) a nice game
   Instead of the very dull word NICE, use these words:
    exciting, sunny, interesting, kind.

67

16

The Magic Skipping-Rope

There was once a little girl who had a magic skipping-rope given to her.

It was a wonderful rope. You took hold of the handles, which were bright red and green with little bells on them, and you said:

> "Standing's dull and walking's slow,
> Skipping's best—and off we go!"

And then you did go off.

You just kept on skipping and skipping. The rope turned by itself; you only had to hold the handles, and it never caught in your feet or in your clothes. It always went on, and you went on too.

When you'd had enough you said:

> "Stop, stop, skipping-rope, do,
> That's enough for me and you."

And then it stopped.

One day the little girl forgot the rhyme that made it stop. I think the skipping-rope must have become annoyed about something. I'm sure it could have stopped if it had tried.

The little girl's father came and tried to take the rope away when he saw what had happened. Strange to say, as soon as he touched his little girl, he began skipping too, jumping up and down, though he had no rope. His wife came and took hold of him, and at once she started to skip also; so did the servant, who tried to stop her mistress; so did their little dog, which jumped up at them. There they all were, bobbing up and down and looking very foolish indeed.

From *Forty Good-Night Tales* by Rose Fyleman

Questions about the Story

A1. Why was the rope a very special one?

2. What did the little girl have to do first of all?

3. What did she have to say?

4. How did she stop skipping?

5. Why could she not stop, one day?

6. What did her father try to do?

7. Why would there always be a noise when the girl was skipping?

8. What do these words mean:

   handles, off we go, annoyed, servant, bobbing up and down?

B1. What was brightly coloured:

   the skipping-rope, the bells, the handles, the dog?

2. How was this rope a magic one?

3. Why was it easy to skip with this rope? Give a long answer.

4. (a) What is not interesting?   (b) What is not quick?
   (c) What is best?   All three answers are in the story.

5. Who were the first, second and third persons who tried to help the girl?

6. How many people looked very silly?

7. This story is (true, possible, impossible, a History story). Which?

8. What is the meaning of:

   magic, wonderful, it never caught in your feet, the rhyme, her mistress, looking very foolish indeed?

Working with Words

1. Write this sentence correctly: what is your little dog's name

2. MORE ABOUT DOING-WORDS

   We saw in Exercise 13 that we say I RUN, HE RUNS, adding an s. Sometimes we have to add ES: I do, he DOES.

69

If the doing-word ends in Y, we have to change the Y to I and add ES:
I try, he TRIES; except after a vowel and y: I pay, he PAYS.
The doing-word HAVE changes to HAS: I have, he HAS.
Make these doing-words end in *s*, *es* or *ies*:

    she push—, he go—, she wash—, it fl—, he limp—.

3. *Puzzle:* Find a doing-word:

    house skip happy hill quickly

4. *Spelling*

These words have a silent B, like thumbs:

    bread-c ——, young sheep (l——), a man who mends burst water-
pipes (pl——), go up a tree (c——), arms and legs (l——)

5. MEET and MEAT

I will *meet* you at four o'clock.
We had cold *meat* for dinner.

Remember: The butcher sells MEAT.

Put *meet* or *meat* into these sentences:

    (i) What kind of —— is this?
    (ii) Buy the ——, then —— me at the bus-stop.

6. If the two words mean the same, write S; if they are opposites, write O:

    (a) neat, tidy (b) hot, cold (c) quick, fast (d) sad, happy
    (e) soft, hard (f) small, little (g) dark, light (h) creep, crawl

7. Choose the right words:

    (i) James (has, as) given me a book. He (his, is) very kind.
    (ii) Please (buy, by) some sweets.

8. Make proper sentences out of the jumbled words:

    (i) would I magic a rope like
    (ii) play on afternoons we games Saturday
    (iii) were late why you morning this

9. What colour are these:

grass, fire-engines, a pillar-box or post-box, fire, summer leaves, autumn leaves, daffodils, soot, polar bears, foxes, oranges?

10. Choose a word from the brackets to make the second pair like the first pair. The first one is done to help you.

father, mother   : grandfather, (home, family, *grandmother*, people)
rope, skipping   : bat, (handles, turning, hitting, flying)
stop, red   : go, (yellow, white, green, blue)
hands, fingers   : feet, (nails, shoes, toes, arms)

11. Use in two sentences: bright red and green   their little dog

Find Out

1. Find out what these words mean:

dull weather, a dull book   he does, a dose   every, very, ever
clip, drip, flip, grip, hip, lip, nip, pip, rip, sip, tip, trip(2), whip
a good answer, a better answer, the best answer   clothes, cloths

Use one word from each group in sentences.

2. *Dictionary Work*

Find these words in your dictionary, then write down the page-number of each one and the meaning given there:

painful, paint, palace, pane, parcel, parents, penguin, people, picnic, purple.

3. GAMES

Make a list of games, with three things about each game, like this:

Football: goal-posts, referee, a football

4. Which one of each pair is SMALLER:

(a) house, palace (b) horse, foal (c) teaspoon, tablespoon (d) giant, dwarf (e) ant, bee (f) horse, pony (g) bookshelf, library (h) small, tiny (i) a packet of salt, a pinch of salt?

17

Tom and the Old Lady

After climbing down the long, steep mountainside, Tom was very tired. He lay on the grass until the beetles ran over him and flies settled on his nose.

He might have stayed there for ever but the gnats and midges took pity on him. The gnats blew their trumpets so loudly in his ears and the midges nibbled so fiercely at his hands and face, wherever they could find a place free from soot, that at last Tom woke up.

He stood up and stumbled on his way, down over a low wall and into a narrow road which led to the cottage which he had seen from the top of the mountain.

It was a very neat, pretty cottage with hedges all round the garden and bushes clipped into the shapes of peacocks, trumpets, teapots and all sorts of things.

Tom walked slowly up to the open door which had flowers growing all round and up and over it. He peeped in, afraid, ready to run away.

Inside sat a smiling, kind old woman with an old cat at her feet and opposite her, on two benches, twelve neat, rosy, chubby little children learning the alphabet.

From *The Water Babies* by Charles Kingsley (adapted)

Questions about the Story

A1. Did Tom go uphill or downhill?

  2. What did (a) the beetles do? (b) the flies do?

  3. (a) What are gnats and midges? (b) Why do we not like them?

  4. Why did Tom wake up?

  5. What had he seen from the top of the mountain?

  6. How many people were there in the cottage?

  7. What animal was there too?

  8. Say what these words mean:

     steep, beetles, settled, nibbled, a *low* wall, a *narrow* road, very neat.

B1. Why was Tom weary?

  2. (a) Did the gnats and midges really *take pity* on Tom? (b) What did they really do?

  3. How could gnats blow trumpets?

  4. Which words in this story tell us that Tom was a little chimney-sweep?

  5. "He stood up and *stumbled* on his way."

    Why does it not say *walked*?

  6. Describe the cottage.

  7. This cottage was a kind of (palace, post office, school, fairy castle). Which?

  8. What is the meaning of:

    a place free from soot, on his way, bushes clipped into the shapes of peacocks, opposite her, benches, neat, rosy, chubby, learning the alphabet?

Working with Words

  1. Choose the right words:

    (i) The mother cat (wash, washes) her kittens very carefully.

    (ii) The sun (dry, dries) the wet streets.

2. LONG, LONGER, LONGEST

a LONG race, a LONGER race, the LONGEST race.

When we wish to say that something is MORE, we add ER:

longer, older, greener

When we wish to say that something is MOST, we add EST:

longest, oldest, greenest

Sometimes we have to make other changes:

(i) Change Y to I and add ER and EST: pretty, prettier, prettiest (except after a vowel and y: gay, gayer, gayest)
(ii) Make double letters first: thin, thinner, thinnest
(iii) If the word ends in E, add R and ST: wide, wider, widest
(iv) Some words change to new words: good, better, best.

Make these words mean MORE and MOST:

loud, high, lovely, tiny, fat, big, brave.

3. SEE and SEA

Tom could *see* a pretty little cottage.   Ships sail on the *sea*.

Remember: SEA is water.

Put *see* or *sea* into these sentences:

(i) Can't you —— that I am busy?
(ii) —— if you can find some —— -shells.

4. Choose the right words:

(i) You do not (no, know, now) the way.
(ii) We are ready for (are, our, hour) supper.
(iii) Did he fall (of, off) the sea-wall?
(iv) Our netball team (one, won) today.

5. *Puzzle:* Find a flower:

bushes   trumpets   beetle   beetroot   tulip   peacock

6. What is the opposite of:

a *narrow* road, a *long* journey, a *low* wall, the *top* of the mountain, pretty, walk *slowly*, *open* door, smiling, kind, *an old* cat?

7. *Spelling:* IE or EI? When it sounds like EE.

   Remember: We usually put I before E, except after C: believe receive

   Spell these words:

   robbers (th . . ves) nose-cloths (handker . . . . . .) above your head
   (c . . ling) great sorrow (gr . . f) savage, wild (f . . rce)

8. What do we call the homes of cows, bees, horses, lions, foxes?

9. Put *a* or *an* in front of these naming-words:

   beetle, gnat, cottage, opening, orange, hour, office, umbrella.

10. Use in two sentences: After climbing down   the open door

Find Out

1. Find out what these words mean:

   his nose, he knows   road, rode, rowed   bush, crush, thrush
   stumble, tumble, rumble, grumble, fumble, mumble, humble,
   crumble, jumble, bumble-bee   hedges, edges   peep, peer

   Use one word from each group in sentences.

2. *Dictionary Work*

   Find these words in your dictionary, then write down the page-number
   of each one and the meaning given there:

   quack, quake, quarrel, quarter, queen, queer, question, queue,
   quick, quiet.

   Remember: Q is always followed by U: QU

3. PEOPLE'S WORK

   What do we call people who do these jobs:

   (a) paint pictures (a——) (b) sell meat (b——) (c) make suits
   (t——)   (d) woodworkers (c——)   (e) sell toothpaste (ch——)
   (f) look after sheep (s——)   (g) look after our teeth (d——)?

4. Which one of each pair is BIGGER:

   (a) cottage, mansion   (b) kitchen, cinema   (c) giraffe, deer
   (d) sword, knife (e) sentence, word (f) path, street (g) crumb, loaf
   (h) mouse, rat (i) tiger, fox (j) brook, river?

18

Stealing Rice

Trumpeter had to be content with a supper of leaves, but that night as he slept, swaying his large head from side to side, he dreamed of the rice fields. When he opened his sleepy little eyes early in the morning, he remembered his dream.

"I will go off and have a breakfast of rice before the others wake up," he said.

The foolish elephant soon found his way back to the fields. He broke down the fence and began to eat the food he loved. He ate, then paused to think, then ate again. He was in no hurry. As he paused to think about his delicious breakfast, he swayed his hind feet backwards and forwards.

Suddenly he felt something close over the foot which happened to be off the ground, and tighten round his leg. Turning in surprise, he saw two brown men. He started to run away, but he soon found himself brought up with a sudden jerk from the rope round his leg.

From *Story Time in the Zoo* by R. K. and M. I. R. Polkinghorne

Questions about the Story

A 1. Trumpeter was a young (boy, elephant, keeper, brown man). Which?

2. What did he dream about?

3. Did he awaken early or late in the morning?

4. What was round the rice fields?

5. What did he keep thinking about in the rice field?

6. What tightened round one leg?

7. What did he do:

ran away, broke free, trampled on his enemy, He could not do anything?

8. Say what these words mean:

swaying his large head, sleepy little eyes, in no hurry, tighten, a sudden jerk.

B 1. Find two things in the first sentence of the story which tell us that Trumpeter was not a boy.

2. Why do you think he dreamed about rice fields?

3. How do we know that the rest of the elephants were still asleep?

4. Why was Trumpeter very silly?

5. How do the words *hind feet* tell us that he was an animal?

6. Why do you think he was called Trumpeter?

7. (a) What did two brown men do? (b) Why?

8. What is the meaning of:

had to be content (satis . . . .), rice fields, paused to think, his *delicious* breakfast, surprise, brought up with a sudden jerk?

Working with Words

1. What are the MORE and MOST words, like LONGER and LONGEST, to go with these words:

early, sweet, hard, big, fine?

2. MORE ABOUT DOING-WORDS

We saw in Exercise 13 that we say this: We run or are running NOW

When the DOING is DONE and ended (in the PAST, not now), we say:

We ran or were running:

I ran or I was running.   He (or she or it) ran or was running
You (or we or they) ran or were running

When the DOING or ACTION is in the PAST, not now, some doing-words end in ED or T: turn, turn*ed*   creep, cr*ept*   hurry, hurr*ied*

Notice how *creep* loses an E and *hurry* changes Y to I.

Some change several letters: fight, *fought*   break, br*oke*

Change these doing-words so that the action happened in the PAST:

He runs, He —— I swim, I —— I feel ill, I —— ill
We keep bees, We —— bees   You carry it, You —— it   They
open windows, They —— windows   She tells tales, She ——
tales

3. ONE and WON

I have *one* sweet left.   We *won* our last match.

Remember: The number I is ONE.   WON is WINNING.

Put *one* or *won* into these sentences:

(i) The Blue team —— the Football Shield.
(ii) We ——·only —— game.

Remember: We win a *game*. We cannot win *somebody*.

I won him in the race.   WRONG
I beat him in the race.   RIGHT

Put *won* or *beat* into this sentence:

The Red team —— the Green team at netball.

4. *Puzzle:* Find a long-necked animal:

elephant, giraffe, chimpanzee, bear, rat

5. Change the ending of these words so that they mean MORE THAN ONE:

night, dream, leaf, rope, church, boy, arch, beach, baby, fly.

6. *Spelling:* Some words have two silent letters: GH, like night.

Think of words with silent GH, beginning with the letter in brackets: (i) up in the air (h) (ii) not heavy (l) (iii) not wrong (r) (iv) not loose (t) (v) hitting, punching each other (f)

7. Write two short sentences, putting *side* in one and *sighed* in the other.

8. Put each describing-word with a naming-word:

Describing-words: red, green, sleepy, front, tight
Naming-words   : leaves, eyes, legs, flames, belt

9. A group of elephants is called a HERD. What do we call these groups: cows, wolves, bees, thieves, singers, sheep?

10. Use in two sentences: dreamed   early in the morning

Find Out

1. Find out what these words mean:

oak *leaves*, Our dog *leaves* no scraps.   hurry, scurry
tighten, frighten   be *content*, a box's *contents*
caw, claw, gnaw, jackdaw, jaw, law, paw, raw, saw(2), thaw
dream, cream, stream, steam, scream

Use one word from each group in sentences.

2. *Dictionary Work*

Find these words in your dictionary, then write down the page-number of each one and the meaning given there:

rabbit, rail, rapid, rat, raw, red, refuse, repair, return, row.

3. WILD ANIMALS FROM OTHER LANDS

Name these animals, beginning with the letter in brackets:

(i) It has a trunk (e)   (ii) A large, fierce ape (g)   (iii) A desert animal (c)
(iv) A roaring wild cat (l)   (v) A white bear (p)   (vi) A striped wild cat (t)   (vii) It jumps (k)   (viii) Like a fierce dog (w)   (ix) Like a striped horse (z)   (x) Like a big, wild bull (b)

4. Which animals make these NOISES:

bray, neigh, bellow, purr, croak, hiss, trumpet, chatter, squeak?

19

Catching Dwarfs

Several thousand Dwarfs dwelt in the caves of the Hartz mountains. They were a great trouble to the farmers, for at harvest-time they used to go into the fields, and steal the corn. No one ever saw them, because they were able to make themselves invisible, by means of their magic caps.

One farmer lost so much corn that he made up his mind to catch the thieving Dwarfs. He placed a rope all round his cornfield, resting it on pegs about three feet above the ground. Then he waited and watched carefully.

After a while, what should he see but a company of little men dancing about in the cornfield and crying out in dismay. When they crept under the rope, it had knocked off their magic caps—and so they were no longer invisible. The farmer caught hold of several of the Dwarfs, and they promised that if he would let them go, they would give him a peck of gold from their treasure store, in return for the corn they had taken.

From *Fairy Tales of Germany* by Barbara Ker Wilson

Questions about the Story

A1. Who lived in mountain-caves?

  2. Whom did they annoy?

  3. How were they a nuisance?

  4. Why did one farmer put a rope round his field? Give a longer answer than "to catch the dwarfs".

  5. Did the farmer catch all the dwarfs? How do you know?

  6. What promise did the dwarfs make?

  7. Do you think the farmer would agree? Why?

  8. Say what these words mean:

  caves, mountains, thieving Dwarfs, pegs, crept under, caught hold, their treasure store.

B1. Why could no one see the dwarfs?

  2. Why did they visit the cornfields *at harvest time*?

  3. Why did one farmer decide to try to catch the dwarfs?

  4. What was his plan?

  5. How tall do you think the dwarfs were, from a clue in the story?

  6. Why did the dwarfs dance:

  for joy, with rage, at a party, to please the farmer?

  7. If you were this farmer, how would you make sure the dwarfs kept their promise?

  8. What is the meaning of:

  Several thousand, a great trouble, invisible, After a while, a company, dismay, a peck of gold, in return for?

Working with Words

  1. Change the spelling of each word in brackets to make it PAST, not now:

  (i) Several thousand dwarfs (live) in caves and (steal) corn.

  (ii) I (swim) across the Baths yesterday.

2. JOINING-WORDS

The dwarfs used to go into the fields *and* steal corn.

The word AND is a JOINING-WORD which we can use to join together two sentences to make one:

The dwarfs used to go into the fields. They used to steal corn.
The dwarfs used to go into the fields and steal corn.

When something happens which we do not expect, something disappointing, we join the two sentences with BUT, not with AND:

I looked everywhere for the lost kitten. I could not find it.
I looked everywhere for the lost kitten but could not find it.

Remember: When we join together two sentences, we can often leave out some of the words, as you have just seen.

Use *and* or *but* as joining-words:

(i) Farmers are very angry about foxes. They try to catch them.
(ii) I ran as hard as I could. I missed the bus.
(iii) We searched everywhere. We could not find our books.

3. HEEL and HEAL

My *heel* is sore. This ointment will *heal* your cuts.

Remember: HEAL means to cure, make better, make HEALTHY.
Put *heel* or *heal* into these sentences:

(i) I wish my cut —— would ——.
(ii) Why is your left —— so red?

4. Make these doing-words end in ING: slip, put, die, fry, come.

5. A farmer works on a farm. What words ending in ER do we use for these workers, beginning with the letter given:

he works in a coal mine (m) mends shoes (c) goes exploring (e) carries luggage (p) sells sugar, tea and cereals (g)?

6. *Puzzle:* Find a shopkeeper:

farmer ploughman chemist shepherd

7. *Spelling*

Some words have a silent G, like sign. Spell these words:

(a) small flying insects (gn . . .) (b) rats can bite like this (gn . .)
(c) a dwarf (gn . . .) (d) Long ago, in the r . . gn of King Richard

8. Put *right* or *write* into the spaces:

Will you please —— the —— answer?

9. Write these sentences correctly:

(i) the river thames flows through london
(ii) john and mary live in victoria street

10. Pick out the buildings:

field, forest, bungalow, table, stable, cinema, flats, pictures, ceiling, lighthouse, school, farmhouse, police-station, shed, garage.

11. Use in two sentences: at harvest time   they promised

Find Out

1. Find out what these words mean:

born, corn, horn, morn, torn, thorn, worn   dawn, fawn(2), lawn
He *saw* a *saw* by the *see-saw*.   great, grate   steal, steel
care, careful, careless   crying, drying, frying, prying, trying

Use one word from each group in sentences.

2. *Dictionary Work*

Find these words in your dictionary, then write down the page-number of each one and the meaning given there:

saddle, sailor, salmon, sandwich, satchel, sausage, scarlet, scratch, shoulder, straight.

3. HOMES

The thieving dwarfs lived in *caves*. Whose homes are these:

an igloo, a house, a hive, an earth, a den, a pigeon-shed, a vicarage, a sty, a burrow, a hutch, a nest?

4. Think of DESCRIBING-WORDS to fit these naming-words (like this: farmer: a BUSY farmer):

rabbit, kitten, tiger, mountains, clouds, fields, lake, storm.

20

The Journey

We are going on a journey,
  We are going all the way,
A-riding in a wagon
  On soft sweet-scented hay:
The Wagoner is waiting
  (A jolly coachman he)
To take us on our journey
  To a farm-house by the sea.

Our great big friends the horses
  Are joining in the fun,
A knowing look they're wearing
  While waiting in the sun;
It's such a jolly farm-house
  In the valley by the sea,
And the farmer's just as jolly
  As any man could be.

There isn't any hurry,
  The ride is splendid sport,
A wood, a windy common,
  Then a little sleepy port.
The farmer's wife is waiting,
  With strawberries for tea,
And cream and smiles of welcome,
  In the farm-house by the sea.

And when the day is over,
  All tired with sheer delight,
We'll climb up to our bedroom
  To sleep away the night
Where linen smells of lavender;
  Then waking full of glee,
We'll hear the farmer calling,
  And murmur of the sea.

Aiden Clarke

Questions about the Poem

A1. The children are going in a (train, car, hay-cart, coach, bus, taxi). Which?

2. What has a pleasant smell? There are two answers, one near the beginning and the other near the end of the poem.

3. Where are they going:

to a camp, farm, stable or school?

4. The weather is (foggy, icy, wet, sunny, frosty, dull). Which?

5. Do the children enjoy the ride? How do you know?

6. What do they have for tea?

7. What can the children hear in the morning?

8. Say what these words mean:

sweet-scented, hurry, full of glee, murmur of the sea.

B1. What is a journey?

2. What is in a seaside valley?

3. Is the farmer friendly or bad-tempered?

4. What do they pass on their journey?

5. How do we know that the farmer's wife is very kind?

6. Is the farmhouse a bungalow? How do we know?

7. How can we tell that the children are very happy at the farm?

8. What is the meaning of:

a wagon, the Wagoner, a knowing look, a windy common, a little sleepy port, welcome, delight, linen smells of lavender? (Can you think why it does?)

Working with Words

1. Make one sentence by using *and* or *but*:

Colin asked me to play in the park. I was too tired.

2. MAKING WORDS SHORTER (See Key to Book One, page 43.)

We can make some words shorter, especially in writing addresses:

St. for Street, Rd. for Road, Mr. for Mister.

We often shorten words when we are talking to someone:

You've for You have, don't for do not, can't for cannot.

Remember: The full stop or the high comma show that some letters have been missed out:

Rd. (Road)   can't (cannot)

What do these shortened words mean:

Ave. Jan. Yorks. Dr. hasn't she'll won't didn't we'll?

3. Change these doing-words to the PAST, like this: I turn, I TURNED:

we look, they sing, you meet, I write, he goes, she eats, he forgets.

4. GREAT and GRATE

A *great*, black shadow

The fire-*grate*

Remember: GREAT means big or important

Put *great* or *grate* into these sentences:

(i) A ——, heavy rock blocked our path.
(ii) The —— is full of ashes.

5. *Puzzle:* Find a meal:

dining-hall   cook   roast-beef   cocoa   dinner

6. Choose the right words:

(i) A (waiter, porter, farmer, grocer) carried our cases at the station.
(ii) My (uncle, aunt, grandmother, niece) is a very kind man.
(iii) (Elephants, Mice, Eagles, Wolves) are enormous animals.
(iv) Young goats are called (lambs, cubs, kids, foals).

7. *Rhymes*

Which words in the poem rhyme with way, fun, sport?

8. *Spelling*

Some words begin with a silent K, like knowing.

Spell these silent K words:

(a) He wore armour long ago   (b) used for cutting   (c) rap on a door
(d) about halfway down your legs   (e) part of needlework

Which letter always follows the silent K?

9. Write s if the two words mean the same; o if they are opposites:

(a) coming, going   (b) all, none   (c) great, huge   (d) mountain, valley   (e) sport, game   (f) begin, start

10. ALL ARE WHAT?

Say what all the things are on each line:

kittens, puppies, ducklings, chickens, cubs
apples, pears, oranges, pineapples
coat, overcoat, mackintosh, skirt
house, stable, kennel, sty
carrots, parsnips, peas, cabbages

11. Use in two sentences: on a journey   the murmur of the sea

Find Out

1. Find out what these words mean:

clear, dear(2), fear, hear, near, tear, year   a berry, bury
would, wood   where, were, wear   This *way*, *Weigh* yourself.

Use one word from each group in sentences.

2. *Dictionary Work*

Find these words in your dictionary, then write down the page-number of each one and the meaning given there:

tab, tablet, tadpole, tar, teach, tent, thaw, thief, tongue, train.

3. BUILDINGS

What are these buildings used for:

barns, garages, cinemas, lighthouses, greenhouses, churches, chapels, banks, schools, fire-stations, police-stations, shops?

4. Think of NAMING-WORDS to fit these describing-words:

terrible, neat, quick, red, heavy, frosty, scared, fierce.

87

21

Scotty

Scotty was a pony, a shaggy little Shetland pony.

He belonged to a boy and a girl who lived in the country, far away from noisy, smoky towns.

They lived in a fine big house with curly twisted chimneys, in a quiet little village miles away from the nearest town.

Behind the house was Scotty's field, with his snug little stable in one corner.

When the sun was shining high in the sky, Scotty walked about in his field and ate the sweet green grass. He listened to the birds and watched people walking by and called, "Whee—ee—ee!" to them.

But when the sun was playing hide-and-seek in the curly lamb's-wool clouds and the cold wind began to puff and blow, Scotty trotted round his field to keep warm.

When the wind blew harder and colder, he galloped round and round; and when the wind was freezing cold and whistled "Whee—oo—whee—oo—ee!" and blew the tiny ragged birds across the sky, Scotty ran into his snug little stable. He shut the door and laughed at the wind.

"Whee—ee—ee!" he said. "Blow, wind, blow. You can't catch me!"

Scotty was a lucky Shetland pony, but he was not really happy. Do you know why?

Because he was LONELY.

From *Scotty, the Lonely Shetland Pony* by E. G. Thorpe

Questions about the Story

A1. What was the pony's name?

2. Where did he live:

   in a city, a small village or a noisy, smoky town?

3. Where was his stable:

   on the lawn, in a corner of a field or in a wood?

4. What did Scotty do when the wind began to blow?

5. Why was he lucky?

6. Why was he sad?

7. Why do you think he called to the people who went past?

8. Say what these words mean:

   shaggy, belonged to, smoky towns, snug, *sweet* green grass, freezing cold, lonely.

B1. Where was Scotty's stable:

   in front of the house, behind it, at the side of it or at one corner of it?

2. Find all the things which Scotty did on sunny days.

3. How could the sun play hide-and-seek?

4. What kind of weather drove Scotty into shelter?

5. Why do you think the tiny birds were ragged (with rough, untidy feathers)?

6. Why do you think Scotty was lonely?

7. Can you think why this *Shetland* pony was called Scotty? (Look at a map of Britain and find the Shetland Isles.)

8. What is the meaning of:

   in the country, curly lamb's-wool clouds, blew the tiny ragged birds across the sky, You can't catch me! ?

Working with Words

1. Shorten these words:

   Street, Saint, August, I am, will not, Lancashire, You have, do not

2. MORE ABOUT DOING-WORDS

   If someone was running in the PAST, not now, we can say RAN, but if we put HAVE in front of it, we must say HAVE RUN:

   I RAN fast but missed the bus. I HAVE RUN fast but have missed the bus.

   Remember: DOING IT NOW   DONE IN THE PAST

I write	I wrote I have written
You begin	You began You have begun
He bites	He bit He has bitten
She breaks it	She broke it She has broken it

   Choose the right words:

   (i) The children (drank, drunk) their milk too quickly.
   (ii) The choir (sung, sang) very sweetly.
   (iii) I have (took, taken) my library book home.
   (iv) The foxes have (went, gone) away.

3. *Spelling:* Some words have a silent w, like wrap.

   Spell these silent w words, all beginning with WR:

   (a) a tiny bird   (b) not right   (c) a way of fighting   (d) part of the arm
   (e) twisting   (f) using a pen

4. Put each doing-word with a naming-word, like this: doing-word: purr; naming-word: cats; Cats purr.

   Doing-words: melts, bark, roar, swim, burns, whistle
   Naming-words: dogs, lions, ice, fire, fish, winds

5. SO, SOW and SEW

   I am not ready, *so* you will have to go without me.
   When are you going to *sow* the peas?
   I will *sew* some buttons onto your shirt.
   Remember: We SOW seeds.   SEWING is needlework.

Put *so, sow* or *sew* into these sentences:
   (i) It is time to —— our seeds.
   (ii) While the girls ——, the boys do woodwork.
   (iii) We worked —— hard that we were tired out.

6. *Puzzle:* Find a word about silence:
   noisy   thunder   crash   noiseless   loud

7. Scotty was a Shetland pony. A pony is NOT a young horse. What do we call a baby horse? (f . . .)   What is a colt?

8. Write three sentences with GOOD in the first, BETTER in the second and BEST in the third.

9. Make these words mean MORE THAN ONE:
   wagon, house, mouse, valley, berry, day, half, shelf.

10. Use in two sentences: noisy, smoky towns   freezing cold

Find Out

1. Find out what these words mean:
   a country, county, the country or the countryside   quiet, quite
   miles, smiles   stables, tables(2)   *Watch* me. Buy a *watch.*
   walking, talking, stalking   sun, son
   Use one word from each group in sentences.

2. *Dictionary Work*
   Find these words in your dictionary, then write down the page-number of each one and the meaning given there:
   ugly, umbrella, umpire, uncle, underground, unhappy, uniform, uphill, useless, usual.

3. TOWN AND COUNTRY
   Which of these are *usually* in towns, which in the country:
   cinema, farm, foxes, cows, Town Hall, car park, forests, skylarks, sheep, traffic, factories, shops, foxgloves, fire-station, lanes?

4. " . . . far from *noisy, smoky* towns."
   Make these words end in Y:
   curl, dirt, mud, anger, greed, juice, soot, stone.

22

Robin Hood

"Five o'clock! Five o'clock! Time to wake! Time to wake!"

A sleek-headed blackbird, perched upon a hawthorn bush very near to Robin Hood's Oak, stopped his morning greeting and preened his feathers in the sunlight, then cocked his black head sideways and peered down at a man who lay, sound asleep, below him, stretched full length upon a bed of moss.

"Five o'clock!" chirped Master Blackbird again.

He flew to the ground beside the sleeping man, pecked and rustled amongst the young green grass; then, with a final twitter, spread his wings and vanished into the trees, as if he would say, "I have no more time to bother with such a lazy fellow!"

A little warm wind swept over the summer woodlands and fanned the man's brown cheek. Robin Hood—for it was he—sighed and stirred softly, then lifted himself upon his elbow, blinking in the sunshine.

From *Greenwood Tales* by Dorothy King

Questions about the Story

A 1. Was it five o'clock in the morning or in the evening?

2. The blackbird was sitting (in an oak, on a bush, on a bed of moss). Which?

3. Why do you think Robin Hood was sleeping *on a bed of moss*?

4. Where did the blackbird go, in the end?

5. Did this happen in spring, summer, autumn or winter?

6. The day was (stormy, wet, sunny, frosty, wintry). Which?

7. Was Robin lazy? *Why* do you say that?

8. Say what these words mean:

sound asleep, chirped, pecked and rustled, vanished, blinking.

B 1. What was the blackbird's morning greeting?

2. How do you know that Robin Hood was not *curled up* on his bed of moss?

3. Why do you think the blackbird pecked in the grass?

4. What does *brown cheek* tell us about Robin?

5. What do you think awoke him?

6. How can the wind *fan* someone's face?

7. What do you think was the real reason why the bird was chirping?

8. What is the meaning of:

sleek-headed, preened (tid . . .) his feathers, cocked his black head sideways, a final twitter, spread his wings, a lazy fellow, summer woodlands, sighed and stirred softly?

Working with Words

1. Which are the right doing-words?

   (i) The stormy wind has (blew, blown) down the elm-tree.
   (ii) The naughty children (did, done) all the damage to the fence.
   (iii) The monitor (rung, rang) the bell.

2. HOW WE DO SOMETHING

Robin Hood sighed and stirred SOFTLY. *Softly* tells us HOW he stirred. He stirred . . . HOW? SOFTLY.

Most words which tell us HOW something was done, end in LY: softly, quickly, slowly.

Remember: He ran SLOW. WRONG
He ran SLOWLY. RIGHT

Put these words into the sentences to tell us HOW something was done:
brightly carefully neatly

(i) Sheila picked up the kitten very ——.
(ii) Early this morning the sun was shining ——.
(iii) If you write ——, you will earn a merit star.

3. BEEN and BEAN

I have never *been* to London.
We have set a *bean* in a jar.

Remember: A BEAN is a plant. has BEEN or have BEEN

Put *been* or *bean* into these sentences:

(i) Only one —— has come up yet.
(ii) Have you —— waiting long?
(iii) It has —— raining during the night.

4. Put these describing-words into the sentences:

clever, angry, bright, rough

(i) The sea was very —— and stormy.
(ii) The park-keeper was —— with the naughty children.
(iii) A —— light was shining across the sea.
(iv) Our dog can do —— tricks.

5. *Spelling*

Some words have a silent H, like where. Spell these silent H words:

a colour (w . . . .) not anywhere (no . . . . .) sixty minutes (h . . .)
for making flour (w . . . t) blowing-noise (w . . . . le)

6. *Puzzle:* Find a red and brown bird:

blackbird   rook   crow   robin   raven

7. Use *and* or *but* to join the two sentences into one:
   (i) The blackbird made a lot of noise. Robin Hood did not awake.
   (ii) The rain poured down. It soaked us to the skin.

8. Put *a* or *an* in front of these words:

sleek-headed blackbird, old blackbird, oak, young man, ugly giant.

9. What do these shortened words mean:

I'm   we're   you're   they're   isn't?

10. *Jobs*
   (a) Who looks after ill people? (b) Who delivers letters? (c) Who owns a farm? (d) Who builds? (e) Who collects our rubbish? (f) Who digs for coal?   (g) Who catches fish?   (h) Who drives a bus?

11. Use in two sentences: vanished   at five o'clock

Find Out

1. Find out what these words mean:

stop, step, stoop, steep   lie(2), lay   flew, flowed
bed, fed, led, red, sped, wed   bread, dead, head, lead, read, tread

Use one word from each group in sentences.

2. *Dictionary Work*

Find these words in your dictionary, then write down the page-number of each one and the meaning given there:

vain, valley, van, vanish, vein, verse, vex, village, vinegar, voice.

3. TREES

Robin Hood's *Oak*. Make a list of wild trees and one of fruit trees.

4. A blackbird perched, stopped, preened, cocked, peered . . .

Make these doing-words end in ED, telling about DOING something in the PAST: step, peep, rustle, fan, grin, stir, hope, hop, cry, hurry.

23

Thomas and Jascha

The house where Thomas lived stood at the end of the village. It wasn't a big house—there were two rooms and a kitchen, a shed and a stable. Like all the houses in this neighbourhood, it had only one storey and an attic. From spring to autumn a family of storks nested on the roof, and in the early morning and in the evening, and sometimes during the day, Thomas heard the storks chattering. In summer there were young ones that you could see quite clearly from the yard. The parents brought them snakes and frogs in their long red beaks, and the young ones strutted about in their nest and tried out their wings.

Thomas often sat on a forked branch of the mulberry tree which grew in the yard, and watched the storks. But on this particular day he would have no time for that, for every Friday he had to go and sell fish with his friend Marko. That is to say, Marko sold the fish and Thomas ran alongside, for he was only ten years old. But his donkey, Jascha, carried the fish-baskets. And no one could manage Jascha as well as Thomas.

From *Jascha* by Franz Hutterer

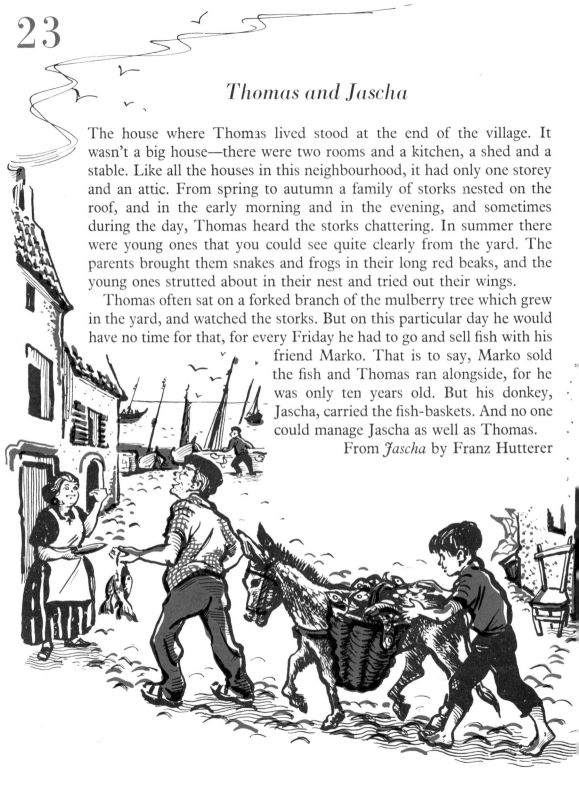

Questions about the Story

A1. Where was the house in which the boy lived?

2. Was it a large or a small house?

3. Where had the storks built their nest?

4. When were the young storks seen: in spring, summer, autumn or winter?

5. (a) Who fed the young storks?   (b) What was their food?

6. What kind of tree grew by the house?

7. How old was Thomas?

8. Say what these words mean:

   kitchen, shed, stable, nested on the roof, chattering, the yard, a forked branch, fish-baskets.

B1. (a) Did this house have proper bedrooms upstairs?   (b) What is an attic?

2. How long did the storks stay on the roof?

3. When did the storks make most noise?

4. Write down the describing-words which tell us about the storks' beaks.

5. (a) Who was Marko?   (b) What work did he do?   (c) When did Thomas help him?

6. Fill the gaps in this sentence:

   "Jascha" is the —— of a book about a ——.

7. Why did Thomas go with Marko:

   He liked fishing. Marko was old and needed help. Thomas could make the donkey behave. He liked donkey-rides?

8. What is the meaning of:

   at the end of the village, one storey, a family of storks, see quite clearly, strutted about, tried out their wings, this particular day, ran alongside?

Working with Words

1. Put these words into the sentences to tell us HOW something was done:

   happily   tidily   quickly

   (i) The pony turned —— and ran back down the road.
   (ii) The children put away their books ——.
   (iii) The kitten played —— with a ball of string.

2. YOU AND I. It is easy to make mistakes with these little words:

   I, me, he, him, she, her, it, you, we, us, they, them, who, which

   Do NOT say: Me and Susan played in the park.
   First mistake: It is not polite to put yourself first. Begin with Susan.
   Second mistake: We cannot say ME played. We say I played.
   No mistakes: Susan and I played in the park.

   Do NOT make mistakes with WHO and WHICH:

   Remember: We say WHO for people and WHICH for animals and things:
   This is the man who won. This is the cat which fights.

   Put *who* or *which* into these sentences:

   (i) I met a man —— had lost his dog.
   (ii) We have a kitten —— is very playful.
   (iii) Do you know a bird —— stays here through the winter?

3. *Spelling*

   There are two OW sounds: One sounds like O (know, blow)
                            The other sounds like OW (now, cow)

   Spell these OW words: (1) like BLOW: black birds (c . . . .) not high (. . .)
   (2) like COW: look annoyed (f . . . . or sc . . .) a circus cl . . .

4. SON and SUN

   The farmer's *son* looked after the sheep.
   The *sun* melted the ice.

   Remember: The SUN is in the sky. A SON is a BOY.

   Put *son* or *sun* into these sentences:

   (i) The —— of a king is called a prince.
   (ii) The —— was hidden behind thick clouds.

5. Write s if the two words mean the same; o if they are opposites:
   (a) huge, large (b) early, late (c) day, night (d) come, go
   (e) dawn, daybreak (f) loud, noisy (g) light, dark (h) light, heavy

6. What are these groups of people: an army, a gang, a class, a crowd?

7. Put these doing-words into the sentences: galloped, creaks, chasing
   (i) The horse —— down the hill, with its owner —— it.
   (ii) The old cottage gate —— on rusty hinges.

8. *Puzzle:* Find a fish:
   donkey   herring   fisherman   trawler   sea

9. What do these shortened words mean:
   wasn't, you're, St. (2), Rd., Dr., I'm, Feb., Wed., Mr.?

10. Use in two sentences: often sat   snakes and frogs

Find Out

1. Find out what these words mean:
   beach, beech, beads, beak, beaker, beam (2), bean, bear, beard,
   beat, beaver   a kitchen, kitten, kite   quiet, quite
   storks, stalks   a yard (2)   I *brought* a book.   I *bought* a book.
   Use one word from each group in sentences.

2. *Dictionary Work*
   Find these words in your dictionary, then write down the page-number
   of each one and the meaning given there:
   waist, wasp, weary, weasel, weigh, wet, whip, whisper, wife, wolf.

3. DAY AND NIGHT
   Put these into their proper order, some being the same time of day:
   evening, dawn, sunset, midday, midnight, afternoon, noon,
   morning, daybreak, dusk

4. Storks eat snakes and frogs. Spell these kinds of FOOD and describe them:
   che . . .   bis . . . . .   bre . .   bu . . . .   ba . . .
   cer . . . .   j . .   me . .   sau . . . . .   fi . .
   veg . . . .   e . . .   su . . .   fr . . .   cak . .

24

Tim Rabbit Meets a Stranger

Tim Rabbit was lonely. Nobody had been near him for a very long time, not since the sun had risen from his bed in the East. He had been out early that morning with several friends, to greet the sun and to dance in those long rays which send away the mists in such a magical way, but that was hours ago.

Everyone had gone on private business, to woods and copses, to secret hollows in the fields, exploring, adventuring, peering through gaps in the walls, poking inquisitive noses round corners, spying at the pony in the croft, the hens in the farmyard, the cows feeding in the fields, so the little rabbit was left by himself.

Tim sat a long time, nibbling some tender young leaves, and thinking deep thoughts. What about an adventure? He might find a friend if he went far enough.

So off he went, across the common, through an open gate, over a field of sweet grass, through a stile, and into another field. Beyond the wall was a cornfield, and at the gate he stopped. A man stood in the middle of the sprouting corn, a fierce-looking, queerly dressed man, with a hat too big, and trousers too short, a coat of rags, and straw sticking out of his sleeves.

From *Ten Tales of Tim Rabbit* by Alison Uttley

Questions about the Story

A1. Who was alone?

 2. What had Tim done hours ago?

 3. What is a secret hollow in a field?

 4. What does this mean:
   poking inquisitive noses round corners?

 5. (a) Where were the fowls?   (b) Where were the cattle?

 6. What did the young rabbit hope to find?

 7. Who was standing in the cornfield:
   the farmer, a soldier, a scarecrow or a clown?

 8. Say what these words mean:
   long rays, private, spying, nibbling, a stile, fierce-looking, queerly dressed.

B1. Why was Tim Rabbit alone?

 2. What does the sun do in a magical way?

 3. What does this notice mean: PRIVATE?

 4. Find five doing-words which tell us what Tim's friends were doing.

 5. Find a word in the story which means little woods.

 6. The pony was in (a secret hollow, a field beside a little farm, a wood, a cornfield, a farmyard). Which?

 7. Why was there a queerly dressed man in the cornfield?

 8. What is the meaning of:
   had risen from his bed in the East, to greet the sun, a magical way, exploring, adventuring, tender, thinking deep thoughts, a cornfield, sprouting corn, a coat of rags?

Working with Words

1. Write these sentences correctly:

(i) Me and Margaret are going to learn to skate.

(ii) This is the boy (who, which) broke your window.

2. PLACES What do we call these places:

Buildings: (a) Where fire-engines are kept   (b) Where films are shown
(c) A kind of money-shop   (d) Where children are taught
(e) Where cars are kept   (f) Its light guides ships past rocks

Not Buildings: (g) rows of fruit-trees   (h) Children play here?

3. DEAR and DEER

That coat is far too *dear.*

Bambi was a young *deer* or fawn.

Remember: A DEER is an animal.

Put *dear* or *deer* into these sentences:

(i) That toy is much too ——, my ——.

(ii) There is a herd of —— in this park.

4. What are the missing words?

A robin is a bird   : A donkey is an ——
We cut paper with scissors: We cut bread with a ——
Trees have treetops   : Houses have ——
Frost, frosty   : Ice, ——
Lions roar   : Lambs ——

5. Use these words in four short sentences: buy,   four,   blew,   bought.

6. *Puzzle:* Find a house:

caravan   den   bungalow   garage   stable

7. *Spelling*

Some words have a silent T, like listen. Spell these silent T words:

(a) a blowing-noise (whi . . . .)   (b) a prickly plant (thi . . . .)   (c) A
very special day: Chr . . . . . . Day   (d) A way of fighting (wr . . . .)
(e) Dry leaves blown along the ground make a rus . . . . . noise.

8. What are the missing words?

GOOD	BETTER	BEST
long	longer	longest
bad	——	——
high	——	——
early	——	——

9. Think of words which are the opposite of:

nobody, a *long* time, early, *smooth* cloth, a *quiet* rabbit, a *heavy* parcel, a *dear* present, a *cruel* master.

10. Use in two sentences: through an open gate   in the farmyard

Find Out

1. Find out what these words mean:

down in a *hollow*, a *hollow* stick   nose, knows   hours, ours
bat (2), cat, chat, chatter, fat, flat (2), gnat, hat, mat, pat, rat, sat
A *stick* was *sticking* out of his pocket.   I *missed* the turning in the *mist*.

Use one word from each group in sentences.

2. *Dictionary Work*

Find these words in your dictionary, then write down the page-number of each one and the meaning given there:

yawn, yellow, yesterday, yolk, young, zebra, alphabet, burrow, currant, dolphin.

3. TIME AND PLACE

Make two lists, one about TIME (when), the other about PLACE (where):

long ago, soon, everywhere, never, over there, in a wood, hours ago, midnight, in a farmyard, dawn, early, nowhere, across a field, now, at five o'clock, by the gate, the riverside, in the road.

4. Which of these words should begin with a CAPITAL LETTER:

rabbit, tim rabbit, a scarecrow, mr. smith, the blacksmith, john, sally, wales, whales, london, pony, scotty the shetland pony?

25

October's Party

October gave a party,
　The leaves by hundreds came—
The Chestnuts, Oaks and Maples,
　And leaves of every name.
The sunshine spread a carpet,
　And everything was grand,
Miss Weather led the dancing,
　Professor Wind the band.

The Chestnuts came in yellow,
　The Oaks in crimson dressed;
The lovely Misses Maple
　In scarlet looked their best;
All balanced to their partners,
　And gaily fluttered by;
The sight was like a rainbow
　New fallen from the sky.

Then, in the rustic hollow,
　At hide-and-seek they played,
The party closed at sundown,
　And everybody stayed.
Professor Wind played louder;
　They flew along the ground;
And then the party ended
　In jolly "hands around".

George Cooper

Questions about the Poem

A 1. Whose party was it?

2. Which tree had yellow leaves?

3. Why did the dancing leaves look like a rainbow?

4. How could the leaves play hide-and-seek?

5. When did the party end:

   at dawn, sunset, midday or midnight?

6. What happened when the wind blew very hard?

7. Which two words describe the party weather:

   dusty, windy, icy, sunny?

8. Say what these words mean:

   a party, gaily, a rainbow, The party closed, sundown, jolly.

B 1. Who were the guests:

   chestnut trees, oaks, leaves, maple trees?

2. How can sunshine spread a carpet?

3. How can Professor Wind lead a band?

4. Why did they dance at this party:

   It was a dancing competition. All parties have dancing. Autumn leaves look as if they are dancing in the wind. There was no room to sit down?

5. Which two trees had red leaves?

6. Why did no one go home after this party?

7. How does October really give a kind of party every year?

8. What is the meaning of:

   The leaves by hundreds came, in crimson dressed, gaily fluttered by, the rustic hollow, Professor Wind *played* louder, "hands around"?

Find out the meaning of:

   All balanced to their partners.

Working with Words

1. What are these places:

lighthouses, laundries, markets, harbours, coal mines, fairs?

2. WRITING LETTERS

37, Green St.,
Langley,
Surrey,
(Post code).
(The date here)

Dear Tony,

I am having a party next Saturday and hope you will come.
Yours sincerely,
Peter

Master A. Brown,
71, Milward Rd.,
NORTHINGTON,
Surrey,
(Post code).

Remember: Start the address HALFWAY DOWN the envelope. Why?

Draw an envelope and address it to a friend.

3. *Puzzle:* Find a tree: daffodil   buttercup   pine   acorn

4. Put in full stops, capital letters, commas and question marks:

(i) tony brown lives in milward road
(ii) have you any stamps please
(iii) at my party we shall have sandwiches cakes and jellies

5. PAIR and PEAR

A *pair* of gloves has been found. May I eat this *pear*, please?

Remember: A PAIR is TWO. A PEAR is a fruit.

Put *pair* or *pear* into these sentences:

(i) I need a new —— of football boots.
(ii) We have two —— trees in our garden.

6. *Spelling*

s often sounds like z: busy. Spell these words in which s sounds like z: (a) lift up (r . . se) (b) small winged insects (fl . . .) (c) long summer hol . . . . . (d) a flower (r . . .) (e) win or l . . .

7. *Rhymes*

Which words in the poem rhyme with name, grand, dressed, played?

8. Think of words which mean the same as these:

grand, lovely, gaily, ended, jolly.

9. Spell the first, second, fourth, eighth and twelfth months.

10. Use in two sentences: like a rainbow hide-and-seek

Find Out

1. Find out what these words mean:

blame, came, fame, flame, frame, game, lame, name, same, tame
by, buy   there, their   new, knew   know, no, now
fine weather, whether He *led* the dancing. Lumps of *lead*

Use one word from each group in sentences.

2. *Dictionary Work*

Find these words in your dictionary, then write down the page-number of each one and the meaning given there:

entrance, fresh, grey, hedgehog, important, jockey, kitten, ledge, murmur, nettle.

3. MONTHS

In which months are these days:

Christmas Day, New Year's Day, the first days of spring, summer, autumn and winter; the summer holidays, Boxing Day, All Fools' Day, Poppy Day? Which month has 28 or 29 days?

4. Put these into two sets, BIG and SMALL:

giants, a pinch of salt, specks of dust, a ton of coal, a pat of butter, mountains, grains of wheat, crumbs, tiny, enormous, a dwarf.

26

The Paper Umbrella

Little Golden Daughter loved the rain, because when it rained she could take out her oiled-paper umbrella that had yellow fishes and blue men and red houses painted on it.

Little Golden Daughter loved the rain because it made soft, pattery noises on her umbrella. It seemed as if the blue men and the yellow fishes were talking to her with the rain for their voices.

There were four little blue men and six little yellow fishes and two little red houses on this paper umbrella. The men seemed to be running very fast, for their legs were bent as if they were hurrying, and their coats were flying open. All the fishes' eyes were rolled to one side as if they were afraid of something, and their bodies were squirmed about into funny shapes.

But the red houses were the funniest of all. They each had six roofs with a little place for windows between, and the four corners of each roof turned up instead of down. There were small golden bells at each corner, and when it rained the bells made sweet singing for Little Golden Daughter to hear. She liked the singing, but she never understood the words.

From *The Chinese Umbrella* by Dorothy Rowe

Questions about the Story

A1. What was the little girl called?

2. Why did she like rainy weather?

3. Where were the yellow fishes, blue men and red houses:

   in the town where she lived; at the seaside; painted on her umbrella; in a picture on her bedroom wall?

4. Fill in the missing words:

   On her umbrella there were two —— —— ——, four —— —— —— and six —— —— ——.

5. Why did the girl think the fishes looked frightened?

6. What were the most amusing things on her umbrella?

7. Why do you think the little girl loved her umbrella?

8. Say what these words mean:

   daughter, soft pattery noises, hurrying, their coats were flying open.

B1. Why do you think the little girl had such a strange name:

   She wore a golden dress. All Chinese names are like that. Her father had a lot of gold?

2. How can we tell that she loved her umbrella?

3. Can you think why her umbrella was made of *oiled* paper?

4. Why did she think that the painted men and fishes could speak to her?

5. Why did she think the men were hurrying?

6. How are Chinese houses different from ours?

7. (a) Where were the golden bells? (b) Were they real? (c) How could they sing?

8. What is the meaning of:

   with the rain for their voices, squirmed about into funny shapes, a Chinese umbrella, "The Chinese Umbrella"?

Working with Words

1. Draw an envelope and address it to your mother and father.

2. MORE THAN ONE

   We have seen how we add S or ES and how some words end in VES or IES when they mean MORE THAN ONE: caps, arches, leaves, babies. Here are some more ways:

   (i) Some words change their middle letters: a man, two men
   (ii) Some have a special ending: one child, many children
   (iii) Some do NOT change at all: a deer, two deer

   Make these words mean more than one: mouse, woman, goose, tooth, ox, sheep, foot.

3. Fill in the missing words:

soft	softer	softest
small	——	-——
——	heavier	——
——	——	funniest
hot	——	——

4. PIECE and PEACE

   Where is my *piece* of red cloth?
   There is no *peace* with you noisy children around me.

   Remember: a PIECE of PIE (begin with PIE)

   Put *piece* or *peace* into these sentences:

   (i) —— is better than war.
   (ii) Who would like the last —— of cake?

5. Put these words into the sentences: on   under   in   near

   (i) Sootikins lay asleep —— the mat —— the kitchen.
   (ii) Look! There's a fish —— that big stone.
   (iii) Snails like to hide —— stones.

6. *Puzzle:* Find a describing-word:

   sky   ape   stormy   wind   run

7. Choose the right words:
   (i) The beggar had (no, none, any) money.
   (ii) I cannot find my book (nowhere, anywhere).
   (iii) The poor robins could not find (no, any) food.

8. *Spelling*

   Some words have the letter L in them but it does not sound like L: walk
   Spell these L words:

   (a) speaking (t . . . . . .)   (b) used on blackboards (c . . . .)   (c) a
   peaceful sea (c . . .)   (d) part of the hand (p . . .)   (e) the stem of a
   plant (s . . . .)   (f) Hymns and Ps . . . .

9. Which has an eye, which has legs, which has hands and which has a
   tongue: a clock   a shoe   a needle   a table?

10. Use in two sentences: soft pattering noises   running very fast

Find Out

1. Find out what these words mean:

   taking, talking   run *fast*, hold *fast*   rain, reins   here, hear, ear
   brain, drain, gain, grain, main, pain, plain, rain, stain, train,
   vain(2)   shade, shake, shame, shape, share, shave

   Use one word from each group in sentences.

2. *Dictionary Work*

   Find these words in your dictionary, then write down the page-number
   of each one and the meaning given there:

   obey, pineapple, quite, right, sharp, twitter, untie, vanish,
   weather, yacht.

3. INSIDE A HOUSE

   Which of these are found inside a house and what are they used for:

   taps, lawn-mower, lamp-shades, light-switches, gate, tool-shed,
   path, bathroom, fences, carpets, drive, tables, wardrobes?

4. Which COLOURS are these:

   a rainy sky, grass, autumn leaves, soot, flames, a cloudless sky,
   a snowstorm, daffodils, snowdrops, oranges, moles, foxes, magpies?

27

The Playful Kitten

One thing was certain, that the WHITE kitten had had nothing to do with it: it was the black kitten's fault entirely. For the white kitten had been having its face washed by the old cat for the last quarter of an hour; so you see that it COULDN'T have had any hand in the mischief.

The way Dinah washed her children's faces was this: first she held the poor thing down by its ear with one paw, and then with the other paw she rubbed its face all over, the wrong way, beginning at the nose. Just now, as I said, she was hard at work on the white kitten, which was lying quite still and trying to purr—no doubt feeling that it was all meant for its good.

But the black kitten had been finished with earlier in the afternoon. So, while Alice was sitting curled up in a corner of the great armchair, half talking to herself and half asleep, the kitten had been having a grand game of romps with the ball of wool Alice had been trying to wind up. It had been rolling it up and down till it had all come undone again; and there it was, spread over the hearthrug, all knots and tangles, with the kitten running after its own tail in the middle.

From *Through the Looking-Glass* by Lewis Carroll

Questions about the Story

A1. Which one had done wrong:

Dinah, the black kitten, Alice or the white kitten?

2. Dinah was (Alice's mother, the mother cat, Alice's sister, a kitten). Which?

3. Why did Dinah rub the kittens?

4. Which kitten was washed first?

5. Where was Alice?

6. What is a game of romps:

rounders, jumping about, bat and ball or skipping?

7. What was full of knots?

8. Say what these words mean:

certain, mischief, paw, hard at work, come undone.

B1. The white kitten had nothing to do with IT. With what?

2. How did Alice know that the white kitten had not been mischievous?

3. What did the mother cat do with her two front paws?

4. Why was the white kitten purring happily?

5. What was Alice doing?

6. Why do you think kittens like a game of romps?

7. Do you think Alice was cross when she saw what had happened? Why?

8. What is the meaning of:

fault, quarter of an hour, rubbed its face all over, *the wrong way*, feeling that it was all meant for its good, curled up, a grand game, the hearthrug?

Working with Words

1. Make these words mean MORE THAN ONE:

   man, woman, a red deer, one black sheep, tooth, child, mouse.

2. OWNING-WORDS

   These words tell us WHO OWNS something:

   my, his, her, its, our, your, their: my coat, your house, their garden.

   Put some of these OWNING-WORDS into these sentences:

       (i) I will lend you —— rubber.

       (ii) The boys are waiting for —— dinner.

       (iii) Are you sure this is —— best work?

3. as white as snow, as cold as ice, as quiet as a mouse, as brave as a lion.
   Put these sayings into these sentences:

       (a) The soldier was ——. (b) You will be caught unless you are ——.

       (c) Mother's washing was ——. (d) Standing in the snow, I felt ——.

4. BEACH and BEECH

   The *beach* was covered by the sea at high tide.
   This *beech*-tree is very old.

   Remember: At the SEASIDE: BEACH   A TREE: BEECH

   Put *beach* or *beech* into these sentences:

       (i) I like a clean, sandy ——. (ii) Is this a —— leaf?

       (iii) The stormy waves thundered down onto the ——.

5. Give each word in List A a word from List B which goes with it:

   List A: butcher, grocer, greengrocer, dentist, plumber, baker
   List B: butter, bread, meat, carrots, toothache, taps

6. *Puzzle:* Find a home:

       rooftop   cellar   coal-shed   pig-sty   garage

7. *Spelling*

   OI often sounds like OY: oil. Spell these OI words:

       (a) very hot water (b . . . . . .) (b) a sound, usually loud (n . . . .)

       (c) earth (s . . .) (d) ruin something (sp . . .) (e) damp (m . . . .)

8. Pick out a naming-word, a describing-word and a doing-word which will *help* you to make up ONE interesting sentence:

Naming-words: children, wind, sea
Describing-words: stormy, happy, icy
Doing-words: played, tossed, howled

9. Make two lists, HOT and COLD:

snow, ice, boiling, freezing, chilly, baking, blazing, sunny, wintry, frost, frozen, fire, January, June, summer, winter, heat, fever.

10. Use in two sentences: white kitten   half asleep

Find Out

1. Find out what these words mean:

for, four   been, bean   by, buy   our, hour   so, sow, sew
as, has   is, his   knot, not   tail, tale   its, it's   piece, peace
dear, deer   band (2), grand, hand, land, sand, stand (2), wand

Use six of these words in sentences.

2. *Dictionary Work*

Find in your dictionary these words which end in OR and write down the meaning you find there:

(i) He acts in plays (ac . . .)   (ii) not rich (p . . .)   (iii) under your feet (fl . . .)   (iv) for shaving (ra . . .)   (v) a looking-glass (mi . . . .)
(vi) seaman (sa . . . .)   (vii) He makes suits (ta . . . .)   (viii) Someone visiting (vi . . . . .)   (ix) heathland (m . . .)   (x) Close the d . . .

3. A BALL OF WOOL

jam, tea, paint, bread, vinegar, scissors, flowers, coal, strawberries, matches

Add one of those words to each of these, like *a ball of wool*:

a box of, a tin of, a pot of, a packet of, a loaf of, a basket of, a bottle of, a bunch of, a sack of, a pair of.

4. Add ING to these words, being very careful with the spelling:

stop, drop, set, slip, dig, put, go, catch, begin, race, come, chase.

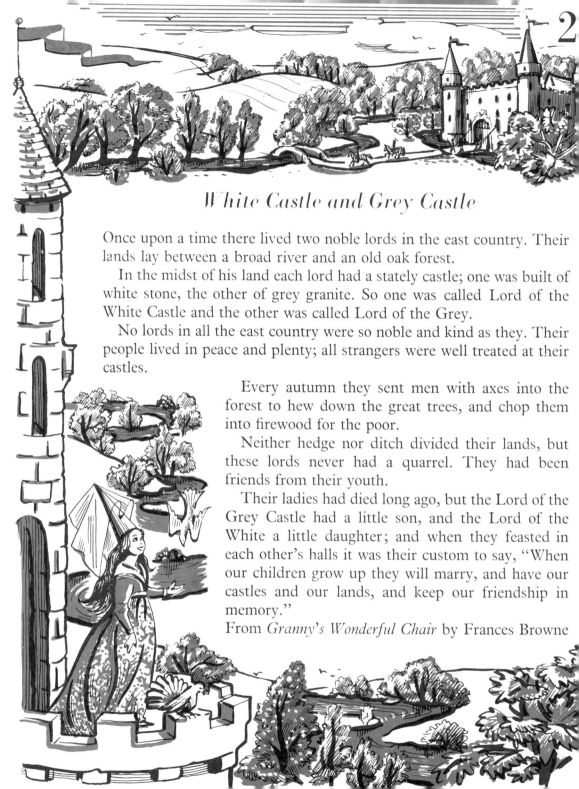

White Castle and Grey Castle

Once upon a time there lived two noble lords in the east country. Their lands lay between a broad river and an old oak forest.

In the midst of his land each lord had a stately castle; one was built of white stone, the other of grey granite. So one was called Lord of the White Castle and the other was called Lord of the Grey.

No lords in all the east country were so noble and kind as they. Their people lived in peace and plenty; all strangers were well treated at their castles.

Every autumn they sent men with axes into the forest to hew down the great trees, and chop them into firewood for the poor.

Neither hedge nor ditch divided their lands, but these lords never had a quarrel. They had been friends from their youth.

Their ladies had died long ago, but the Lord of the Grey Castle had a little son, and the Lord of the White a little daughter; and when they feasted in each other's halls it was their custom to say, "When our children grow up they will marry, and have our castles and our lands, and keep our friendship in memory."

From *Granny's Wonderful Chair* by Frances Browne

Questions about the Story

A 1. Who lived in the east country?

  2. What were the two castles made of?

  3. Why did the two lords have special names?

  4. The lords were (cruel, enemies, kind, quarrelsome). Which?

  5. What did the two lords do to visitors:
     kill them, rob them, welcome them or drive them away angrily?

  6. Why did they send men into the forest in autumn?

  7. Finish this sentence:
     The two lords had been friends since . . .

  8. Say what these words mean:
     Once upon a time, a broad river, axes, strangers, firewood, hedge, ditch, quarrel.

B 1. What was on one side of their lands? What was on the other side?

  2. What do you think a stately castle is :
     white, grey, important-looking, ruined?

  3. Which word in the story is the name of a very hard rock?

  4. What does this mean:
     Their people lived in peace and plenty?

  5. What did the two lords hope might happen, one day?

  6. What does "keep our friendship in memory" mean?
     (Our children are friends. They will always remember that we were friends. Our friends will visit us. I have a good memory.)

  7. What *might* the two lords have quarrelled about? (Look at the fifth paragraph.)

  8. What is the meaning of:
     noble lords, an old oak forest, In the midst of, well treated, hew down, Their ladies?

Working with Words

1. Use these three words in sentences of your own: their, our, its

2. MORE ABOUT OWNING

    Granny's Wonderful Chair

    Granny's: The high comma tells us about OWNING.
    Who OWNS the chair? Granny. She is the OWNER of the chair.
    We put this after the OWNER: 's
    Granny's wonderful chair   John's shoes   Mary's blazer   a bee's wings

    If the OWNERS are MORE THAN ONE and already end in s, we just add
    the high comma: the horses: the horses' tails   boys: boys' coats

    Use the high comma to show the owners:
    (i) The little cubs nose was sore.
    (ii) My fathers new tie is bright green.
    (iii) At the Horse Show all the horses tails were tied with ribbons.

3. BEAR and BARE

    The polar *bear* dived into the icy water.
    The sun will burn your *bare* shoulders.

    Remember: A BEAR is an ANIMAL.

    Put *bear* or *bare* into these sentences:
    (i) The big, brown —— was looking for food.
    (ii) A —— is a big, strong animal.
    (iii) The cat scratched my —— foot.

4. Make these words mean more than one:
    woman, country, river, castle, goose, hedge, ditch, lady, child.

5. *Puzzle:* Find a town: England   Liverpool   Australia   America

6. Put these words into the sentences to tell us HOW something was done:
    sadly   swiftly   happily
    (i) Three little fox-cubs were playing —— in the wood.
    (ii) The lost dog wandered —— over the hills.
    (iii) Hawks can fly ——.

7. Which words are right?

    (i) Do you (no, know, now) my name?

    (ii) The shepherd (knew, new) where his dog had gone.

    (iii) The playful kitten fell (off, of) the chair.

8. What are these places:

    castle, greenhouse, cinema, chemist's shop, Bank, cow-sheds, orchards, hutches, cottages, bungalows, libraries, flats?

9. *Spelling:* OUGH can be said in several ways:

    It sounds like UFF: rough, tough   It sounds like OO: through

    It sounds like OW: bough, plough   It sounds like OFF: cough

    It sounds like O: though, dough

    Learn the spelling of all these words.

10. Use in two sentences: a broad river   a quarrel

Find Out

1. Find out what these words mean:

    a fire, fire a gun, a fire-engine, firemen, firelight, a fireplace, the fireside, firewood, fireworks   were, where, wear   here, hear, ear   there, their   poor, pour   to chop, a chop

    Use one word from each group in sentences.

2. *Dictionary Work*

    Find these WORKMEN, all ending in ER, in your dictionary and write down the meaning you find there:

    ba...   car......   fa....   gar.....   kee...   mil...

    shop......   tea....   wai...   war...

3. FURNITURE

    Make a list, like table, bed, wardrobe.

4. What do we call the MEAT from these animals:

    pigs (3: b....   h..   p...)   sheep (m.....)   cattle (b...)?

    Spell these DRINKS:

    co...   co....   t..   lem.....   m...   wa...

29

David's Secret

"What have you found?" asked the stranger.

David hesitated, wondering if he should share his secret. But the man was so close that he could see the wolf, and there seemed no reason to pretend. So he said, "It's a wolf."

"A wolf!" said the stranger. "My! let's have a look." And he came closer and looked down at the small, red animal. It was lying down again, as happy as a kitten, while David rubbed its stomach.

"Do you think it's all right?" he asked.

The stranger said: "Why not? Looks fine to me. But I'll let you into a secret."

"A secret?"

"Yes. I'm sorry to say your wolf isn't a wolf at all."

"Isn't it? Why not?"

"It's a fox—a fox cub. Probably about ten weeks old, I'd say. The vixen—that's its mother—must be somewhere near. She was probably moving it. They don't usually leave them for long, but she won't come close while we're here. What are you going to do with it?"

From *Foxy* by John Montgomery

Questions about the Story

A1. What question did the stranger ask David?

2. What was David's answer?

3. What was the little red animal doing?

4. Why do you think it was so happy?

5. The little red animal was a (wolf, wolf-cub, fox-cub, kitten). Which?

6. How old was it?

7. Why did its mother not come back for it?

8. Say what these words mean:

stranger, a secret, Foxy, pretend.

B1. What was David's secret?

2. What was the stranger's secret?

3. How do you share a secret or let someone into it?

4. Why do you think David thought the little animal was a wolf?

5. What is a vixen?

6. Why do you think the mother was moving the cub?

7. What would you do if you found a wild fox-cub in the woods?

8. What is the meaning of:

hesitated, no reason to pretend, probably, rubbed its stomach?

Working with Words

1. Use the high comma to show the OWNER:

    (a) Davids secret (b) The strangers secret (c) The cubs mother
    (one cub) (d) The mother of three cubs: The three cubs mother

2. SPEECH MARKS

    "What have you found?" asked the stranger.
    Notice how we put Speech Marks " " round the words spoken by the
    stranger. Look at all the other spoken words in the story about David's
    Secret. Notice how all the spoken words go inside Speech Marks: " "
    Put Speech Marks round the spoken words:

    (i) David said, I am going to take it home.
    (ii) What are you doing in my field? the farmer shouted.

    Remember: Put full stops, commas and question marks inside the Speech
        Marks: "Where are you going"? I asked. WRONG
            "Where are you going?" I asked. RIGHT

3. *Puzzle:* Find a tool:

    tablecloth hammer road city cupboard

4. Join the two sentences on each line by using *and* or *but*:

    (i) I went to the library. It was closed.
    (ii) I went to the library. I chose an exciting book.

5. *Spelling:* Think of the missing SILENT letters:

    si . n   autum .   coco .   g . ard   . night   . onest   crum . s

6. ALL ARE WHAT? Say what they all are on each line:

    John, David, Peter, Alan, Christopher
    Carol, Christine, Brenda, Elizabeth, Valerie
    Smith, Jones, Brown, Robinson
    England, Scotland, Wales, Ireland

7. LYING and LAYING

    The cub was *lying* down.   Mother is *laying* the tea-table.

    Remember: LYING is when we LIE down.
            LAYING is when we PUT things down.

Put *lying* or *laying* into these sentences:

    (i) Why are you —— down?

    (ii) I found a kitten —— on the ground.

    (iii) Our hens are not —— many eggs lately.

8. Make these words mean more than one:

    secret, wolf, animal, kitten, fox, thrush, half, baby, boy, chimney.

9. "Do you think it's *all right?*" he asked.

    Remember: ALL RIGHT is TWO words. There is no such word as *alright*. Use *all right* in a sentence of your own.

10. Make these doing-words end in ING: swim, hit, race, share, rub.

11. Use in two sentences: a small red animal   a secret

Find Out

1. Find out what these words mean:

    bare, blare, care, dare, fare, flare, glare, hare, mare, pare, rare, share, square, stare   no, know, now   wonder, wander

    It's a wolf with a thorn in *its* tail.   *close* the door, *close* to the door

    Use one word from each group in sentences.

2. *Dictionary Work*

    Find in your dictionary these words which end in ON and write down the meaning given there:

    (a) Sta . . . . (police or railway) (b) Blow it up (bal . . . .) (c) A fierce, fiery dra . . . (d) Sit on a cus . . . . (e) I . . . is heavy. (f) A bitter, yellow fruit (l . . . .) (g) Very many (mil . . . .) (h) A bird (pig . . .) (i) A tin of sa . . . . (fish) (j) Do not drink poi . . .

3. ZOO ANIMALS

    Make a list of zoo animals, like wolves and lions.

4. Think of ten words telling HOW something was done, to go with these doing-words (like *run* QUICKLY):

    fly, crawl, write, speak, shout, listen, fasten, fight, shine, scowl.

30

Bed-Time

The evening is coming,
   The sun sinks to rest;
The rooks are all flying
   Straight home to the nest.
"Caw!" says the rook, as he flies overhead;
"It's time little people were going to bed!"

The flowers are closing;
   The daisy's asleep;
The primrose is buried
   In slumber so deep.
Shut up for the night is the pimpernel red;
It's time little people were going to bed!

The butterfly, drowsy,
   Has folded its wing;
The bees are returning;
   No more the birds sing—
Their labour is over, their nestlings are fed;
It's time little people were going to bed!

Here comes the pony—
   His work is all done:
Down through the meadow
   He takes a good run;
Up go his heels, and down goes his head;
It's time little people were going to bed!

          Thomas Hood

Questions about the Poem

A1. What time of day is it in the poem:

morning, afternoon, evening or night?

2. Where are the rooks going?

3. What do they say?

4. Why are the flowers closing?

5. (a) Are the birds noisy or quiet? (b) Why?

6. What are nestlings? You can work this out from clues in the third verse.

7. What is the pony doing?

8. Say what these words mean:

rooks, he flies overhead, meadow, pimpernel, The sun sinks to rest.

B1. Which of these words could we use instead of *little people*:

ladies, ponies, butterflies, children, fairies, flowers?

2. Which three flowers are asleep?

3. "The bees are returning"

(a) Where do you think they are going? (b) What do you think they have been doing?

4. What work do you think the pony has done?

5. "Up go his heels, and down goes his head"

(a) What is he doing? (b) Why?

6. Find in the poem:

(a) a bird (b) an animal (c) two insects

7. Is the poem about spring, summer, autumn or winter? How do you know?

8. What is the meaning of:

Straight home, buried in slumber (fast asl . . .), drowsy, labour (very hard w . . k), folded its wing, takes a good run?

Working with Words

1. Put in Speech Marks to show which words were SPOKEN:
   (i) Caw says the rook It's time you were in bed.
   (ii) What time shall we go? I asked.

2. GROUPS

   We have special names for groups of things, like a *swarm* of bees and a *flock* of sheep. What do we call groups of:

   cows, puppies, wolves, birds, ants, ships, flowers, cards?

3. WERE, WHERE and WEAR

   We saw in Exercise 6 that *where* is a place, like *here*.

   Remember: We WERE doing something. We WEAR clothes.

   Put *were*, *where* or *wear* into these sentences:
   (i) —— did you say you —— going on holiday?
   (ii) What shall we —— at the party?

4. *Puzzles*

   Find a colour: blind, purple, cart, reading

   Find a workman: sheep, farm, shepherd, field

   Find a noise: hit, click, door, nose

   Find a fruit: beech, peach, beach, reach, teach

   Find a place: John, park, lark, jackdaw, fish

5. *Learn*

   The proper names for (i) naming-words: NOUNS
                        (ii) describing-words: ADJECTIVES
                        (iii) doing-words: VERBS
                        (iv) how-words: ADVERBS

6. Change the ending of the verbs so that something happened in the PAST, not now, like run, I *ran* or I *have run*:
   (i) The visitors (say) they were sorry to be late.
   (ii) I (see) you hit that little boy.
   (iii) Have you (find) out who (do) it?

7. *Spelling*

Spell these broken words:

My aunt and u . . . .   My mother and f . . . . .   My sister and b . . . . . .   Have you p . . . the bill?   "Come here!" he s . . .   angr . . .   to the naughty boys.   A glass of wa . . .   Fr . . . . s, not enemies   Four, fourteen, fo . . y

8. Put capital letters, full stops, commas and question marks into these sentences:

(i) will you come with me

(ii) birmingham is a big city

(iii) i like apples plums pears and peaches

9. What is the difference between these noises made by dogs:

barking, growling, howling, yapping and yelping?

Fill in verbs to tell the noise made, like this: Rooks CAW:

Donkeys ——, Cats ——, Robins ——, Frogs ——, Horses ——, Lambs ——.

10. Think of the words which mean the same as:

little, closing, drowsy.

11. Think of the opposites of:

coming, little, closing, asleep, shut, here.

12. Use in two sentences: straight home   through the meadow

Find Out

1. Find out what these words mean:

sun, son   rooks, brooks   flower, flour   heels, heals bring, cling, fling, going, king, lying(2), mowing, moving, ring, sing, sling, spring(4), sting, string, swing, tying, trying, wring.

Use six of the words in sentences.

2. *Dictionary Work*

Find in your dictionary any ten words which begin with these letters, then write down their meaning:

awa—— bea—— cor—— dea—— ech—— fai—— gan——
hea—— ide—— jac——

3. ANIMALS, BIRDS, FISH OR INSECTS

Put these creatures into four lists:

fox, herring, ant, eagle, owl, badger, cod, bee, frog, rhinoceros, rook, plaice, greenfinch, gnat, goose, giraffe, vixen, swallow, sparrow, fly.

4. Think of VERBS to fit these adjectives and nouns, then make up eight interesting sentences:

Angry lions   The playful puppy   A frightened baby   A brave dog
The tired man   The busy gardener   Fierce wolves   The lost lamb